PRAISE FOR *JIMMY DYKES: THE FILM DOESN'T LIE*

"As a college basketball coach, I'm constantly watching film. We review film every day in an attempt to get better because the film never lies. It reveals who we really are—both individually and as a team. I've long admired Jimmy Dykes—not only as a leader, communicator, and coach, but also as a man of faith. In *Jimmy Dykes: The Film Doesn't Lie*, Jimmy masterfully communicates the importance of evaluating where you are in crucial areas of your life. This is a must-read for anyone pursuing a life of conviction, bold determination, stronger relationships, and a more authentic walk with the Lord."

—RICK BARNES
UNIVERSITY OF TENNESSEE HEAD BASKETBALL COACH

"Jimmy Dykes' voice, stories, and challenges to men comprise a compelling vision that men will want to reach in their lives. *Jimmy Dykes: The Film Doesn't Lie* is a prime-time read."

—DR. RONNIE FLOYD
PRESIDENT OF THE SOUTHERN BAPTIST
CONVENTION EXECUTIVE COMMITTEE

"Eye control is one of the main fundamentals when developing players at all levels of the game of football. The same can be said about daily life. Every day men are hit with distractions that keep our eyes off of what's most important—our relationship with Christ. In *Jimmy Dykes: The Film Doesn't Lie*, Jimmy adds needed focus in our pursuit of a real God."

—GUS MALZAHN
AUBURN UNIVERSITY HEAD FOOTBALL COACH

Jimmy Dykes: The Film Doesn't Lie is a passionate, practical, and entertaining guide for anyone pursuing authentic manhood. Jimmy not only delivers interesting anecdotes from his playing, coaching, and broadcasting of college sports, but he also brings wisdom from the scripture and authentic passion while fixating on loving God and his family."

—DR. SAM HANNON
CONGREGATIONAL LEADER, FELLOWSHIP
BIBLE CHURCH OF NORTHWEST ARKANSAS

"Truth is revealed when the process of evaluation is worked through. It's true in business, athletics, and certainly in our personal life. *Jimmy Dykes: The Film Doesn't Lie* will draw you to search your heart in key areas that can be holding you back from a deeper, closer, more authentic walk with God. This book will challenge you, change you, and open your heart to a God who loves you."

—ERIC J. POERSCHKE
MANAGING PARTNER AND CHIEF STRATEGIC OFFICER,
NEXTLEVEL THINKING

"As a basketball coach, watching film is a key part of that process. Film reveals the truth, and embracing that truth leads to change, growth, and improvement. *Jimmy Dykes: The Film Doesn't Lie* allows you to take an honest, open look at your life and wholeheartedly pursue God with genuine passion and conviction. Jimmy speaks to your heart about accountability and striving to get better every day in our walk with Christ."

—CUONZO MARTIN
UNIVERSITY OF MISSOURI HEAD BASKETBALL COACH

"If you are looking to grow as a man of God, this is a must-read for you. Jimmy is a man after God's own heart. From his family to his platform as a college basketball analyst for ESPN, Christ is seen woven throughout his life. He has a strong passion for reaching men and taking their walk deeper with Christ. Get ready to search your heart and allow God to work in the depths of your soul. You will not be left the same."

—DR. NOE GARCIA
SENIOR PASTOR, NORTH PHOENIX BAPTIST CHURCH

THE FILM DOESN'T LIE

THE FILM DOESN'T LIE

EVALUATING YOUR LIFE
ONE PLAY AT A TIME

JIMMY DYKES

TRIUMPH
BOOKS

Library of Congress Cataloging-in-Publication Data

Names: Dykes, Jimmy
Title: The film doesn't lie : evaluating your life one play at a time / Jimmy Dykes.
Description: Chicago : Triumph Books, 2020. | Summary: "This is an inspirational guide of how to live one's life while using basketball as a template"—Provided by publisher.
Identifiers: LCCN 2019049834 (print) | LCCN 2019049835 (ebook) | ISBN 9781629377902 (hardcover) | ISBN 9781641254427 (ebook)
Subjects: LCSH: Dykes, Jimmy—Religion. | Basketball—Psychological aspects. | Self-actualization (Psychology)—Religious aspects—Christianity. | Christian life. | Basketball coaches—United States—Biography.
Classification: LCC GV884.D94 A3 2020 (print) | LCC GV884.D94 (ebook) | DDC 796.323019—dc23
LC record available at https://lccn.loc.gov/2019049834
LC ebook record available at https://lccn.loc.gov/2019049835

This book is available in quantity at special discounts for your group or organization. For further information, contact:

Triumph Books LLC
814 North Franklin Street
Chicago, Illinois 60610
(312) 337-0747
www.triumphbooks.com

Printed in U.S.A.
ISBN: 978-1-62937-790-2
Design by Meghan Grammer

To every person who reads this book, know that God loves you. He cares for you more than you could know. He is for you, not against you. He can change your heart like he has mine...

Everyone thinks of changing the world, but no one thinks of changing themselves.

—Leo Tolstoy

CONTENTS

FOREWORD

Jimmy Dykes started work at ESPN shortly after I did in 1995. Though we didn't meet for a while, his voice on the air created an instant connection. After all, we were fluent in similar dialects and colloquialisms. Beyond the dulcet southern tone, his voice also carries an urgent sincerity. I soon came to know that isn't Jimmy's television persona; it's who he is. Sincere. Urgent. Compassionate.

When he and I would talk at our college basketball preseason seminars or get assigned to call games together, I was always struck by Jimmy's complete comfort in talking about how he had prayed about a decision or his desire to use his opportunities and platform to glorify God. There were also times during our conversations that he'd say something like, "At first, I didn't want to listen. I resisted, but God showed me."

That's sort of like watching the film. As broadcasters for ESPN, often we don't want to watch the film, though it's more likely digitized video these days, but it's still the recording of what we've done on air. The discipline of re-watching a film will magnify imperfections. It can be uncomfortable. Even the perfectly delivered line or expertly captured moment in a broadcast comes with the potential of making us too proud. But we know better—or at least we should. The stumble, the hurried word, the missed opportunity—it's coming. It'll be right there on the film. It always is. It's the same way with evaluating our lives, too. The temptation is just: don't watch, don't do it. Why subject yourself to that type of scrutiny? Because it's the only way to get better. But you only improve if you're willing to measure yourself against the proper standard.

Jimmy's standard is his faith and what God's written word says. When he and I shared breakfast prior to going to a Duke practice on the morning of February 12, 2019, the conversation turned to living our convictions in a worldly profession. Jimmy shared with me how God was teaching him about key areas in his life like forgiveness, the power of our spoken words, and the importance of obedience in our life.

Obedience is not always the most popular concept in our culture. Yet the Bible teaches us in the book of Ecclesiastes that obedience is the whole duty of man. We talked about the lasting impact of our words, particularly sharp or thoughtless words that can have a lasting impact, especially on those closest to us. I shared with him—probably for the umpteenth time— how I struggle with worry. He listened and said he would pray for me in that area. I knew he would.

There we were in a hotel lobby having a heart-to-heart conversation about a real God and an authentic walk with Him. We had no idea we were just a few hours away from witnessing Duke's comeback against Louisville—maybe the most memorable comeback of the 2018–19 college basketball season. And as memorable as the game was later that night, to me the witness for God that we shared with each other about our vulnerabilities, our sin, and our need to joyfully share the mercy God has shown us with others had an even greater impact.

For me that often means finding the courage to share my faith with others and not hide behind the idea that maybe this isn't the right time. It's like putting off watching the game film or the tape of the show. But the reality is: the areas of failure or imperfection are there. It's encouraging to have someone who understands, fights the same battles we all do, and is willing to watch your film with you. The time to do it is now, and this book, *Jimmy Dykes: The Film Doesn't Lie*, will challenge you, change you, and reveal a God who loves you deeply.

I see Jimmy Dykes live with consistency, courage, compassion, empathy, and humility. He possesses a great awareness of the standard needed to find success. More accurately, how finding success is truly defined by giving our lives to Christ and what that looks like as we are going on our paths on a daily basis. II Corinthians 13:5 encourages us to examine ourselves to see whether we are in the faith. Jimmy's walk constantly encourages and challenges me to do that. I trust that you will be similarly inspired. Only by studying the film from the game will we be—in Jimmy's words—"hard to guard."

—*Rece Davis joined ESPN in 1995 and was named the host for ESPN* College GameDay, *the network's flagship college football program, in February 2015. In addition, he is the prime host of the network's on-site coverage for both the College Football Playoff and the NCAA men's Final Four. The host of ESPN's* College GameDay *basketball road show, he also calls Thursday night basketball games, following the completion of the football season.*

Chapter 1

EVALUATE YOUR FILM

Any man's life will be filled with constant and unexpected encouragement if he makes up his mind to do his level best each day.

—BOOKER T. WASHINGTON

WRITING THIS BOOK has changed much of what I thought I knew about the direction of my life. What I truly value has been reorganized and I now see differently. Areas I was blinded to, I can now see. What my heart pursues has been replaced by a new aim—and a different target. The importance of how I treat others and lead my family has grabbed me by the shoulders and shaken my core. Words like forgiveness, obedience, balance, and toughness have a different meaning and effect on my life. I have greater awareness and a deeper understanding for phrases like "surviving a drought," "knowing God's voice," and "guarding my tongue."

A God I thought I knew met me in the quietness of my heart and revealed to me more clearly who He is. The need I had for Him has gone from conditional to desperate. The complacency in my life toward God has been exposed, and the self-centered mind-set I have carried around my entire life has been weakened and redirected. Needless to say, I did not see this coming. My heart desires a faith that is so tested, so proven, and so authentic that all of hell cannot shake it. I am not there yet, but I am certain of where I am trying to go.

I have learned through the school of hard knocks that the only way lasting change can ever come about is by a constant submission to God. Whatever amount of will, grit, discipline, or toughness I tried to muster up in the past to bring change into my life is now secondary to knowing that only God—and making myself humble before Him—will produce the changes I so desperately need.

I have not won the battle in any area. I am making strides, gaining ground, and taking steps forward, but I have not won.

My focus is on improving, and that will remain an ongoing process throughout the rest of my life. Like many of you who have picked up this book, I simply desire to get better at how I live life. Over the past 25 years of my broadcasting career with ESPN, I have seen unlimited examples of teams and individuals with that same goal. They are striving to improve at what they do.

Simply getting better is easy to write and easy to say but is difficult to do. The discipline, determination, and energy that it takes to pull it off is unique, but it's common ground to those who rise above the norm. Every winning team, high-achieving individual, thriving company, or difference-making organization I have ever been around for any length of time has one thing in common. They are driven by an unquenchable thirst to get better. Winning at what they do is certainly a goal, but it's not *the* goal. *The* goal is to improve at what they do. Winning is a by-product.

The final score is not what drives top level performers. They understand that who wins and who loses is often determined by things they ultimately cannot control. A missed call by an official late in a game, an injury at a key point in the season, or the competition simply being superior are things that cannot be controlled.

There is always another mark to hit or level to obtain if the intention is to simply improve. Wins may certainly come when those new standards are reached, but for high achievers, winning does not change the daily goal and laser focus of who they are and how they work. Possessing a constant awareness of how to improve, finding that answer, and ultimately acting on that answer is what separates average from excellent in all walks of life. A focus on winning can make you complacent. A focus on improvement can make you zealous.

Over the past two-and-a-half decades of covering college and professional sports for ESPN, I have witnessed the high cost of complacency countless times. It is a killer in sports, business, education, relationships, and a pursuit of a life changed by God. Getting lulled into a hazy gray fog that disguises the road as being clear can end in devastating ways. That's what makes the emphasis on improving different than the emphasis on winning. A focus on winning will conceal your deficiencies and can camouflage the problems. A focus on improvement will expose your faults and magnify your weaknesses.

I want to open your eyes, your thoughts, and your heart to the potential harm a slow fade to complacency can cause to any area of your life. Satisfaction, a false sense of security, and smugness are all dangerous slopes. I have observed countless teams and individuals falling from the mountain of favor to the valley of failure all because they became prideful in how they went about their days, allowing arrogance and ego to take command, and they ultimately lost that unquenchable desire they once had to get better.

Perhaps you are in a season of elevation right now in one of those big chapters of life. Your marriage, children, job, health, daily purpose all are at a high level and rising. Your closeness to God is as intimate as it has ever been, and your walk with Jesus is becoming more authentic and real to you every day. I hope that is the case for you.

Or maybe you are winning in key areas of your life right now more than you are losing, but deep down you know the opponent—whatever that may be—is making a serious run and you now find yourself just trying to hold on to the lead. I realize some people are okay with just being okay. Perhaps it doesn't concern you that in some crucial areas of your life where you once were winning by 30 or 40 points is now down to a two-point game. But I don't think that's who you are. I believe most people are wired to want more, obtain real change, and to live with greater purpose. Simply getting better every day is common ground and an area of agreement for those who are consistently moving forward in their lives and refusing to settle for the common path.

So what does getting better really look like? You cannot give the correct answers if you aren't asking the correct questions. A pivotal part of pursuing improvement is taking the time to properly evaluate. Every successful team I have ever covered as an analyst for ESPN makes the process of evaluation a regular part of their routine. When it comes to sports, nothing impacts the evaluation process more than film study. Truth is revealed for teams when discerning, skilled, intentional, laser focused eyes break down and study a practice or game film. This type of detailed evaluation process will bring forth an accuracy and veracity about any team or individual. When change and advancement are the goals, few things are more crucial than the process of appraisal. Nothing can impact you more than searching for answers to what the concerns are and what the issues are on the path to simply getting better. If this evaluation process is done correctly, it can be a difficult and painful action. Unfortunately, hard stops most people. But if you want to make progress, you cannot run from hard.

Hall of Fame coaches, world-class athletes, Olympic coaches, flourishing business owners, powerful CEOs, and many other highly successful people are masters at evaluating.

Nothing goes unchecked, and nothing gets taken for granted. They are not discouraged by hard. They remain sharp, alert, and hungry for excellence. People who experience growth in life take action as opposed to reacting to life. They do not run from hard and they are comfortable being uncomfortable.

Some of my most enjoyable moments as an analyst for ESPN occur when I am given the opportunity to sit through a film review with a coaching staff and their players. Before this film session occurs, I can tell you that every coach on that staff has watched the entire film multiple times. For a college basketball staff, six to 10 people have put their eyes on a film multiple times, identified the problems, and made adjustments to fix those problems.

A college football coaching staff of 20 to 30 guys will have their eyes on every single play of a four-hour game. Think about that for a moment. We are talking hundreds of hours committed to the evaluation process of a game that only has 60 minutes of actual playing time. That speaks clearly to the importance of evaluations. Individually, those coaches will watch a single play multiple times from different angles in their office late into the night, and as an entire staff, that's the first thing they do the next morning. Everyone in the room is searching that film with a trained eye, making detailed notes, determining why something is happening, and highlighting what will be discussed with the entire team and individual players. Everything is open for evaluation and critique at this point. It does not matter if the film they are grading was a game that resulted in a win or a loss. The evaluation process does not change. Coaches are searching for ways to get better. Improvement is the goal—plain and simple.

After these film evaluations are completed by the coaching staff, more times than not, an edited version of the game or practice is presented to the players. Some coaches prefer to show these graded film clips in the order they occurred during the game. Others will show the positive plays first and plays that need correcting second. Every head coach has his or her way of doing things, but the goal is the same for all: improvement. LSU football coach Ed Orgeron refers to the team's film sessions as "Tell the Truth Mondays." That is the day of the week set aside for the entire team to watch the previous week's game film. Truth is revealed, teaching points are made, and strides to improvement begin.

I have noticed over the years that winning teams with great culture, humble pride, and mature discipline watch their game film with a strong purpose. Film study is a respected time during a team's daily and weekly schedule. There is limited conversation as players and staff enter the film room. From the opening moment in that meeting room, a sense of focus, accountability, and eagerness to learn is felt. In most team film rooms, players are in assigned seats based on position, depth charts, or classification as a student. Cell phones and headphones are not allowed. Notebooks are out, and full attention is given to the film and the coach leading that film session. The room goes to another level of intensity every time the head coach interrupts to make a point or teach a concept. The voice of the leader carries the most weight.

I have learned a great deal about hundreds of teams just by watching them watch film. Caring teams, disciplined teams, confident teams, and ultimately winning teams watch film differently than selfish teams, undisciplined teams, complacent teams, and losing teams. I can say the same thing from observing individual players in terms of how they watch film, respond to correction, and sit through those difficult times of teachable moments. Those individuals, who are soft, selfish, and possess a less coachable mentality, look at feedback as an attack on their feelings and blame others for their downfall. Those with a humble spirit and a desire to improve view accountability as a necessity, not an assault. Those players learn, grow, and prosper. Mature, winning players understand the fact that…the film doesn't lie.

Film reveals truth, and embracing that truth is what leads to sustainable change, growth, and improvement. What shows up on any game or practice film is the authentic version of who you are as a player and who you are as a collective team. What you thought you did as a player on certain plays may or may not match up with what the film shows. Who you think you are as a player may look nothing like how you really are performing. You are what you do—not what you say you are doing—and the film will confirm this one way or the other.

You cannot correct those areas you are unwilling to confront, and any film session done correctly will include moments of confrontation. The evidence will clearly be shown on film, questions will be asked between coaches and players, answers will be demanded, and teaching will be accomplished.

Few things at the collegiate or professional level are more difficult to endure than a two-hour film session with both players and coaches in attendance. The actions, attitudes, decisions, and efforts that show up on film are clear and convincing. The film session becomes even more painful if that game film they are watching resulted in a loss. Every missed assignment, example of poor body language, and lack of execution or intensity is shown and thoroughly dissected. For a player watching this kind of film in this type of setting, there is no place to hide and no excuses to be made. *The film doesn't lie.* The good and the bad are clearly visible to everyone in that room. What must be corrected is obvious to all. Having won or lost that particular game is not the heart of the issue. The purpose is to stalk the problems and change what needs changed.

The most successful coaches I know, the ones who consistently win and have the ability to get everyone around them to perform at their highest level, have a few things in common. One of those prevalent traits is being brutally honest in their evaluations. Praise is given when it is earned, and losing efforts are called out in front of the entire room. There is a high degree of nonnegotiable accountability in those meetings. It is sincere, direct, and straightforward. The idea is: *I love you enough to confront you with the truth.* The standards and expectations for how a coach believes his team should perform are made crystal clear to everyone in that room. Film evaluations are challenging at times if done correctly, but they are absolutely necessary.

If highly successful teams, athletes, companies, and organizations take the time to evaluate on a consistent basis, why are we hesitant or even negligent to do so in our own personal lives? There is no way of getting around it. Real change can only occur after what needs to be changed has been clearly defined. If it's true for any team, individual sport, organization, or Fortune 500 company, it's true for you and me. If we want advancement, growth, breakthrough in our lives, we must take the time to pinpoint those areas where we are negligent, lacking, and being defeated.

There is considerable benefit from evaluating our lives in a similar way to how coaches and top CEOs look at their teams. You cannot allow winning and what that looks like to you to mask the problem areas and overshadow those things you need to deal with in your life. I invite you to begin looking at your life as a game or practice film that you are grading like a coach and needs to be analyzed, scrutinized, and prioritized. If graded properly, that film will have much greater value than a team improving, a company making more sales, or a brand expanding in impact.

This is about you and your life. Your path, your trajectory, and ultimately your destiny can all be altered by what you choose to see or ignore on your film. As a result, expect this process at times to be difficult, eye opening, encouraging, and heart changing. Don't shrink from this moment. Simply ask God to prepare your heart as we begin this journey.

I get great insight into what a team is truly made of by observing the practice that occurs immediately following one of those grinding film sessions. Practice is where the evaluation becomes an action. Those areas that were exposed, taught, and dealt with on film now come to life. Teaching points are executed for long stretches at a time. Intentional effort is made to ensure that mistakes seen on film are not repeated. Words become actions, and momentum toward progress begins to take place. Some things are quick fixes, and some are not, but the process is in motion and is continuous. Perfection is the goal—even if it is unattainable.

So where does all of this fit in with you and me? Why invest time into a discipline that is difficult? How will that bring change into my life? Why should we grade our lives like a coach grades a film? What is to be gained by asking God to search us and change us from the depth of our souls? Why should you be concerned if your heart is stagnant, your pursuit of God is complacent, and your hunger to know Him is gone? What's the big deal if the enemy has your eyes in a fog and on a slow fade to a destination you never intended to go?

I love the book of James in the New Testament of the Bible. The author has a call-it-like-it-is style that speaks directly. In the book of James, we are given more insight as to how and why this evaluation process is beneficial and necessary when it comes to seeking change in our lives. James 1:22 says, "Do not merely listen to the word and so deceive yourselves. Do what it says."

That is so clear, honest, and straightforward. It is so important to listen to what God's word says, but it's equally important to obey and to "do what it says." This principle from the Bible is going to hold up in your life in every area. It does you no good to evaluate if your actions do not change.

Don't deceive yourself and ignore those things God may speak to you about. Search your heart and ask God to open your eyes to what is undeniable on your film. What are those things that need to be identified in your life in an honest, straightforward, and possibly hard-to-watch fashion? Why are you losing in key areas of life, and just as important, what is occurring on a regular basis that—if not dealt with—has the potential to change a win into a loss?

I encourage you to place boundaries in your life and understand the importance of having non-negotiable standards to live by. Take a hard look at the balance or lack thereof in your life right now. Examine the power of your words. Perhaps there's something or someone you need to walk away from, something that is keeping you distracted and missing God's best for your life. Is there any form of unforgiveness, greed, or bitterness starting to take root in your heart? Maybe you are in the middle of a long stretch of difficult, confusing, burdensome days in your life, a drought of some sorts. How are you handling those tough times?

You need to watch your film. No one else needs to be in the room—just you and your film. How honest and transparent will you be with yourself and with God is the key. I know it may be difficult to watch, and you may have to watch multiple times before you see what you need to see. But false evaluations are worthless, and fake film sessions are of no use. If you watch with unfiltered eyes and an open heart, you will know the film doesn't lie. It never has and it never will.

The most successful coaches and consistent teams fix the problem now. They do not wait until the next day, next week, or next season. There is an obvious determination and discipline to fix the problem right there in the middle of the battle when the game is being decided. Isn't that where we are? Right in the middle of the battle? Your battle may look a little different than mine, but we are all fighting something.

Begin asking God for the same determination and culture that these types of teams have. That determination and culture are what sets them apart, makes them unique, and enables them to grow through difficulties. They do not resist coaching. There is no agenda other than team success and consistently seeking out ways to improve. There is an urgency about winning teams that is hard to define but easy to see. They fix the problem before the problem costs them success, and we must do the same in our own life as well.

I have come to the conclusion over the years that below average coaches can't even see the problem with their teams. Good coaches can see the problem, but they cannot fix the problem. And great coaches can identify and fix the problem. That is our goal as we go through this book. Think of yourself as a coach. You are coaching you. Begin asking God to open your eyes, remove the fog, and grant you the ability to see what He desires for you to see. Secondly, ask for God's power for change in your life in the form of a more determined mind-set, a more disciplined life, and a heart that is renewed on knowing God and His love for you.

Resolve to no longer give the enemy power in your life due to complacency, laziness, pride, or disobedience. Trust that God will clearly speak to your heart and show you what needs to change. Ask Him to give you an unquenchable desire to improve in those things He reveals to you. He will do it. And when He does, thank Him and be grateful God loves us enough to not leave us stuck in a place that is less than His best for us.

I am not encouraging you to watch your film for the purpose of beating yourself down and losing your confidence. No coach, who wants success for his or her team, watches film with their team with that type of agenda. Do not let the fear of guilt keep you from progress. I sense some of you will have to overcome that fear and press on. Others may feel like it's all they can do to make it to the next day because life is happening so fast that the enemy has you distracted, and seeking God and searching your heart may seem nearly impossible to pull off. That is a subtle lie from the enemy. Reject that thought and move on.

For others, complacency has possibly steered you off course. Some of you may occasionally give a passing thought to an area of concern, but deep down that unquenchable thirst to know God and to hear His voice is just not there. You see plays on your film that have the potential to derail you or cost you the entire season, but those plays are being rationalized, ignored, and excused.

Understand that you are not the only one who watches your film. The enemy (Satan) studies your film and knows your tendencies better than you do. He creates a gameplan based off what your film reveals. Highlighted in his notes are areas of vulnerability he can attack and cracked doors he can bust open. You are the opponent in his mind, and he is after you.

I have heard a statement similar to this said countless times by coaches, trainers, and those in some type of leadership position all across the country: "If I'm not pushing you, demanding more from you, challenging you, and holding you accountable every single day, then ultimately I'm cheating you."

God rewards effort. He has promised to draw near to those who draw near to Him. One of my favorite moments in the Bible occurs in chapter two of Mark when Jesus rewards the effort of a paralyzed man. In that story Jesus had returned to his hometown of Capernaum and was teaching inside a home. We are told that a paralyzed man was carried on a mat to that house by four men in hopes of seeing Jesus and being healed. By the time they arrived, there were so many people who had come to hear Jesus speak that the gathering of people overflowed outside the house, and a standing room-only crowd was in attendance. It was obvious that the path to Jesus was not going to be easy that day. This paralyzed man, however, had decided to pursue change his life. He was determined to walk again, and no crowd, no obstacle, no hardship was going to keep him from getting where he knew he needed to be.

Fighting through the crowd and getting inside that home through the front door was not an option. Instead, those four men, who were carrying the paralyzed man, somehow managed to lift him to the roof of the house and began digging a hole. Once the opening in the roof was large enough, the paralyzed man was slowly lowered down while lying on his mat into the presence of Jesus, where he was ultimately healed, and his life was changed.

That paralyzed man and his friends understood the same thing we all must grasp. God rewards effort, and He is faithful to those who seek Him. There are times in life that you may have to rip a hole in a roof in order to get closer to God and have an authentic walk with Jesus for the first time in your life.

Remember those actions, priorities, attitudes, and decisions that are going to show up on your film are an accurate reflection of who you are and where you are going. God's written word is full of those things we all desire. We love His promises of eternal life, healing, and blessings that come our way in many forms. We all need the promises of God and we all need the obedience. This is a call to both.

It's that unquenchable thirst to get better that will ultimately determine change in your life. Let's get started. Dim the lights, turn on your film, and start taking notes. Watch your film with your eyes and grade your film with your heart. No matter what you may come across, know that God loves you unconditionally. Let's get to work.

Chapter 2

· COMMITMENT

Hardships often prepare ordinary people for an extraordinary life.

—C.S. Lewis

I N THE SUMMER of 2011, God clearly laid on my heart a vision to organize a one-night rally for men of Northwest Arkansas. That desire blossomed into a night where we saw over 1,500 men from all walks of life come together to be challenged by testimony from normal, everyday guys, who had personally witnessed God work in authentic ways in their life. It was a powerful night, and God's Holy Spirit was at work. Marriages were saved, relationships with family members were restored, addictions were broken, and a fresh call to obedience was felt by many. I still hear stories today of men who asked Jesus for forgiveness that night to restore their purpose as men and renew their hearts for Him.

I listened to many narratives of how God had worked in someone's life as we prepared for that rally. As the event was being organized, our goal was finding seven or eight different men to share their stories in a 10-minute time frame. Over numerous morning coffees, lunch appointments, and phone conversations, I spoke to many of those men.

I specifically recall one of those lunch appointments when I sat across from a man I was meeting for the first time. I had been told through a mutual friend that this guy had a powerful testimony of a fall from favor and the power of prayer. I listened closely as he described his journey. For about 15 minutes, I listened intently to a man who had seen his life unravel due to disobedience, selfish choices, eyes distracted from God, and ears that ignored God's warning. I heard a story of a man who lost his wife, his family, his job, and ultimately his fear of God all due to allowing the enemy an opened door, being unfaithful in his marriage, and making self-destructive decisions. He spoke with remorse and regret over the times he had straight out told God, "I don't care. I'm doing this anyways."

After explaining how his life had completely hit rock bottom, he then began explaining how God had moved in his life. As he finished his thoughts on how God had restored his path, his marriage, and his job, I will never forget the one statement he made at the end. "I owe a great deal to my wife, who, unknowing to me at the time, marched around our home every single day for the months that we were separated, praying with our children that God would change my heart and bring me home," he said.

A wife and a mom who had been dealt a bad hand refused to give up. Her commitment to prayer and claiming the promises from God in her life was dependable, persistent, and unchanging. I am certain that doubt tried to creep in as days turned into weeks, and weeks turned into months for that praying wife. But one woman's commitment to trust God for the results overwhelmed the doubt.

I love hearing stories of commitment. I don't hear enough of those type of stories. Commitment is a basic, fundamental area we must dive into as we watch our film. That word—commitment—has expanded in my own life over the past several years. I have listened to, read about, and witnessed that word being played out in multiple ways through multiple scenarios. Over the past several years of my life, I had thought I had known the definition of the word commitment and then one day I met a young man named Eddie Martin.

It was the morning of December 29, 2006, in Charlotte, North Carolina, the day before the Meineke Car Care Bowl game between the United States Naval Academy and Boston

College. As part of our normal preparation for the broadcast, our ESPN crew assigned to that game met with both coaching staffs and individual players that day to make certain we were completely dialed in on both teams. I was told by our game producer that Navy had a player who was currently battling cancer and that I needed to visit with him to learn his story. I will never forget that 20-minute conversation on the field of Bank of America Stadium, home of the NFL's Carolina Panthers.

As Eddie was introduced to me, I could tell immediately by his firm handshake, purposeful eye contact, and "Sir, it's nice to meet you" tone that this young man was different. I simply asked, "Would you please tell me your story?" And for the next 20 minutes, I listened, I laughed, I cried, I asked myself questions, and, ultimately, I grew as a man.

At the age of 21 on the first day of fall practice just over four months earlier, Eddie told me he had been diagnosed with stage-three Hodgkin's lymphoma. A tumor the size of his fist was lodged inside his abdomen with no option of surgery to remove the cancerous growth, as surgery had a high risk of death due to the location of the mass. Additional cancer cells had expanded throughout his neck, chest cavity, and pelvic region. The rigorous schedule of the academy and constant mental and physical exhaustion that becomes the norm for every plebe on that campus most likely disguised his symptoms longer than normal.

Eddie had been recruited as a quarterback out of high school but had made the switch to slotback and special teams for his junior season. He had played in every Navy football game the previous year. But on this morning instead of preparing to battle Boston College the next day in a football bowl game, he was battling to stay alive.

He described to me how every two weeks for the past four months, he would receive his chemotherapy treatments on Friday. I could hear in his voice how painful and difficult those treatments were on his body. He described how it took every fiber of strength in his body and every ounce of will in his heart to stand at attention on Monday mornings at 6:30 AM during those special instruction periods that are required for all men and women at the academy after having received chemo treatments on the previous Friday afternoons. I felt his fight and determination when he talked about refusing to let what he was battling be an excuse for not meeting the daily requirements that every other Navy brother and sister had at the academy. I can still hear the disappointment in his voice as he talked about watching his teammates practice over those past four months while he sat on the sidelines.

On a bench in an empty 75,000-seat stadium, I was having a real conversation with someone who was in a real battle for his life. It was sobering and powerful. I can still see the pride in his eyes as he explained to me that the Navy players had selected him to carry the United States flag out of the tunnel and onto the field before every football game, an extremely high honor for any service academy athlete. I sensed that carrying that flag about 50 yards from the tunnel to the sidelines equated to a healthy person running a 26-mile marathon. It took everything he had to accomplish that task.

It was obvious to me I was visiting with someone who had been and still was going through hell. Life had hit him right square in the face at the age of 21. It was unlike any conversation I had ever had, and that's not just limited to college athletes or coaches.

As I reflected on all that he was sharing with me, I kept going back to something he stated early on. He told me that after being diagnosed with cancer, the Naval Academy informed him he should leave the academy and return to his hometown of Cantonment, Florida, so he could concentrate all of his efforts on this fight for his life. He was encouraged to step away, withdraw, abandon the path, and go fight his battle at home. "But sir, I chose to stay," he said.

After finishing his story, I asked him one simple question: "Eddie, why did you stay?"

He paused briefly, looked me squarely in the eyes, and responded, "Because, sir, I had made a commitment."

"A commitment to what?"

"A commitment to all of my Navy brothers and sisters, a commitment to my team, and a commitment to my country," he said. "And nothing, sir, will ever take me away from that commitment. I signed up for something bigger than me and I'm going to die trying to complete my senior year and graduate from one of the greatest institutions in the United States."

I didn't really know how to respond. I just knew that I would never view the word commitment the same again. I told him I would pray for him and that I would do my very best the next day to tell his story to a national TV audience on ESPN. He simply replied, "Thank you, sir, I greatly appreciate you taking the time to visit with me."

A couple of hours after that conversation with Eddie, I was handed a sheet of paper detailing the daily schedule for every young man and woman at the Naval Academy, including Eddie as he was fighting his battle with cancer over the previous four months. As you read through this daily routine for all men and women at the United States Naval Academy, note that many Midshipmen do not actually go to sleep until closer to 1:00 AM due to extra studies or just a few minutes of personal time. It's a great challenge to the strongest of young men and young women, including Eddie.

Naval Academy Daily Routine

6:30–7:00 AM	Special instruction period for plebes
7:00 AM	Morning meal formation
7:15 AM	Morning meal
7:55–11:45 AM	Four class periods of 50 minutes each
12:05 PM	Noon meal formation
12:10 PM	Noon meal
12:50–1:20 PM	Company training time
1:30–3:30 PM	Fifth and sixth class periods
3:45–6:00 PM	Varsity athletics, extracurricular activities, and personal activities, including drill and parades twice weekly in the fall and spring
6:30–7:15 PM	Evening meal
8:00–11:00 PM	Study period
12:00 AM	Midnight Taps for all midshipmen

Navy lost that football game the next day 25–24 on a last second 37-yard field goal as time expired in front of 52,000 fans, but a young man on the Navy sidelines by the name of Eddie Martin had impacted me greatly. I have stayed in touch occasionally with Eddie over the years. And it gives my heart great joy that his cancer has been in remission for more than 13 years now. He still serves our country as a lieutenant commander in the United States Navy, is married, and just recently became a father for the second time. He shared with me recently that, "there comes a time in our lives that we may feel all is lost, but if we just continue to fight and put our trust in God, He will deliver in some form or fashion."

I think about Eddie every now and then when I hear of someone backing out of a commitment. When I see college athletes transfer at a ridiculously high rate because things aren't going like they thought they would, it's too hard, or the coach is too tough, I think back on that conversation inside that stadium that morning. When high school athletes give a verbal commitment to a particular school regarding where they will attend college yet continue to take official visits to other universities and college campuses, I know the word commitment is thrown around with very little conviction these days.

I think about him when I hear of a marriage breaking up or a dad who is no longer engaged with his family because of a hobby or other distraction. Not everything that gets your attention deserves your attention. Let that resonate for a minute.

When I see people lose their grip on God's hand and walk away from what they know is God's truth in their lives, I realize the word commitment is merely a word—if not backed up with actions. That conversation I had with Eddie often crosses my mind when I hear of a promise broken or a business deal falling apart because someone backed out of his or her word. And I wonder what Eddie would tell them if he had the opportunity to sit with them like he did with me inside an empty Bank of America Stadium back in 2006.

I believe we would all benefit from pausing every now and then to reflect on that word commitment. I know I would. We have all given our promise to something. Let's cut right to the chase and address it head on. Are you a faithful husband or wife? That is a yes or no question…period. On a scale of 1 to 10, what does your film reveal about your commitment to obedience when God clearly speaks to you? We dedicate our children to God at a young age. We commit to raising them in a home that honors God and gives Him the rightful place He deserves. How is that commitment looking on your film right now? When you answer yes to someone, does it really mean yes, or does it mean yes unless something better comes along? Or yes if I still feel like it when it's time to follow through? When you tell someone you will pray for them, do you really pray for them or have you simply fallen into that standard response that is popular to use when someone shares a concern with you? When we see on social media that someone responds with: "Thoughts and prayers for you," are they faithful to their word?

Do you know how to persevere, press on, stand firm, and be single-minded for what you signed on for? At some point that's what it's going to come down to when honoring a vow. You give your word to something or someone. It gets hard, and now you have to endure. Trust me: at some point in your life, you will have to just hold on. As you evaluate your film right now, maybe that's exactly where you are. You may be holding on with all you have to save your marriage. Perhaps you are standing firm in prayer to turn your kids away from some outside influence that's relentlessly trying to take them down. It could be that you are bearing a physical hardship similar to the one that Eddie was engaged in.

Someday you may look up and find yourself in a trial that is so burdensome, so confusing, so unfair, that you begin to doubt God, and your trust and commitment in Him comes into question. I cannot tell you what your commitment test will be. If you are not currently in one, it's just a matter of time until that test is staring you right in the eyes. And when it does happen, your resolve to fight will determine if you have any chance to hold on, persevere, and watch God's hand move in your life.

I have seen words like fight, commitment, and resolve played out time and time again through competition on an athletic field or court. I have also witnessed those words impacting an individual in actual life battles, the kind of battles that do not make sense and test a person's faith to the depths of their soul.

Some of the most resilient, faithful people I know are not athletes and do not get their name written in the sports page or talked about in a postgame press conference. But I would put their fight and understanding of commitment up against anyone. One of those people in my life is Becky Patterson.

My wife and I have known Becky for several years now. We met through her affiliation with the Fellowship of Christian Athletes. As I began writing this chapter on commitment, her name and story would not escape my thoughts. I was hesitant at first to contact her, not knowing what she would say to the request. I just knew if I was going to give an example of fight and real-life hardship, her story needed to be included.

We talked on the phone late one afternoon, and I made the request for her to share some thoughts with me on trials, tests, and the commitment to fight when the hard times hit. She said she would have something for me by the next day, and like all tough people do, Becky delivered. Here is her email to me just as I received it.

From: Becky Patterson
To: Jimmy Dykes
Date: Monday, August 19, 2019 01:34 PM CDT

Coach...Obviously I'm not an author and this is pretty rough but I know you are on a time crunch. I am thankful to the Lord that you thought of us. Jesus used you to encourage me and I am humbled. I will not be offended if you don't share my story... like I said, I am blessed that you thought of our family. Keep loving your girls...BOTH of them!

I got pregnant on the night of my high school graduation. My boyfriend, Chris, and I married shortly after although he was only starting his senior year of high school. It is only by the grace of God that we are still married today...preparing to celebrate 27 years together.

When our daughter Micayla, was five years old, my mother who was my best friend, lost her lengthy battle with breast cancer. When I was 29, I myself was diagnosed with breast cancer. I had to have a double mastectomy and chemotherapy. Exactly one year after my treatment ended, I was diagnosed with cervical cancer and had to have a radical hysterectomy. During that time, Chris and I became custodial parents of an athlete I met through my work with the Fellowship of Christian Athletes. At age 29, we became instant parents again, to a 16 year old young lady.

By the time our daughter Micayla entered high school, we felt like we had been through quite a bit in our young married lives. We truly felt as though we were living the dream. I loved my work with FCA and were blessed to watch our daughter look up to college athletes who were walking with the Lord. We traveled around the country with AAU basketball and led Bible studies in hotel rooms where girls would open up the Word, encourage one another, and soak up the truth.

When August of 2010 rolled around, we were walking into Micayla's senior year, preparing for college. On September 3rd, Micayla and three of her friends went to a John Mayer concert in Tulsa, Oklahoma. It was the first time in 17 years of her life that we allowed her to go out of town without one of us. We received videos and text messages throughout the concert and she called to let us know they were headed home. A few hours later, there was a loud knock on our door. When Chris opened the door, he was greeted by two police officers who stood in our doorway. They told us that our daughter had been involved in a vehicle accident and that she did not survive. As I shared earlier, challenges and adversity had not been uncommon but this was a life-changing blow. Micayla was a hilarious, joy filled teenager with a bright future ahead of her. She was a high school athlete standing 6 foot tall and was preparing to play her last year in high school. She was smart, witty and talented and her laugh was contagious.

Our home was always filled with teenagers...MY TEENAGER. She was my life. NOW WHAT?

Jimmy, it's hard to actually put into words how those next few days, weeks, and months unfolded. I know that love and support we received from our community helped me put one foot in front of the other. That being said, I know that the power of prayer and the Holy Spirit interceding on my behalf so that I could have the strength to be obedient is what kept me on track to keep fighting the good fight. (Fight the good fight of the faith. Take hold of the eternal life to which you were called when you made your good confession in the presence of many witnesses. 1 Timothy 6:12)

I had to find a quiet place to be with the Lord every day. It still gives me goosebumps to think about the tangible ways that He spoke to me. He told me the battle was just beginning...it was about to get hard. When people started getting on with their own lives, mine was still at a complete standstill. My flesh wanted to gnash my teeth and run. Run anywhere but home...and how quiet and lonely inside of those walls were. Yet, every day I fought the temptation to abandon the faith that had carried me through becoming a teen mom, losing my own mom, and my own battle with cancer.

I go back to that time and remember feeling as though I was a soldier in training. I was in the middle of a battle and knew I would not win if I didn't suit up every day and train. I was not going to win the battle if I was passive or sat back and waited for somebody else to fight. I had to fight. The enemy wanted to see me crumble in my despair, walk away from the ministry of FCA and drown in depression.

I had authentic conversations with God for the first time in my life. I cried. I screamed. I kicked and spit with anger quite often. Then, as children do with their earthly parents, He would calm me down and comfort me in my grief. The Lord told me to wait. He was close enough that I knew I could trust Him but I wasn't very patient. Yet I waited.

God very clearly told me to wait for one year. Deep down in my soul I hoped that He was going to take me out of my misery and let me come join Micayla in heaven. He had other plans. One year and five days after the accident, I received a phone call from a young lady who had found out she was pregnant and asked if my husband and I had considered adoption. Nine months later we brought home a newborn baby boy that we named after my husband. Christopher is now seven and is filling those same empty rooms with joy. Where there once was silence, there is now laughter. Every promise the Lord ever made to me He has fulfilled. He's never let me down. There have been challenges and trials in the past seven years but I run back to the truth that has carried me through every valley I've walked through.

Trust in the Lord with all your heart and lean not on your own understanding: in all your ways submit to Him and He will make your path straight. Proverbs 3:5-6

Now I want to ask you again: where are you with that word commitment?

Our word, our promises, our convictions are all doable and easily kept when it's rolling our direction. In every area of life, hard beats most people. It stops them in their tracks, it distracts them by offering up easier options, and it keeps many from a breakthrough and blessings that God has waiting for them on the other side. Is hard beating you right now? A very difficult situation, circumstance, bad break, or bad choice could have you wavering on what to do and how long to hold on.

I don't know if I will ever understand and execute the word commitment in my life like Eddie and Becky have done in theirs. I wish my commitment to pray and trust God 100 percent with His promises was as bold and courageous as that praying wife for her husband at the beginning of this chapter. I do know I am thankful for those people who have crossed my path and opened my eyes to what a massively important word commitment is. Words of honor, vows, and promises—those plays will be easy to identify on your film. What will you do?

Chapter 3

THE SPOKEN WORD

Raise your words—not your voice. It is rain that grows flowers—not thunder.

—Rumi

WOKE UP AT 6:00 AM on the morning of February 12, 2019, in my hotel room in Louisville, Kentucky, with great anticipation and excitement for the day. I remember thinking that in just more than 15 hours I would be on the call for the college basketball game later that night between the No. 2-ranked team in the country, the Duke Blue Devils, on the road to face the No. 16 team, the Louisville Cardinals. It was a primetime game on ESPN during the middle of February between two of college basketball's premier programs. Those are the type of match-ups—as an announcer—you hope live up to the hype. And it certainly did. Duke-Louisville delivered an instant classic to a national TV audience and a sold-out KFC Yum Center crowd in the heart of downtown Louisville.

Rece Davis was my play-by-play partner for the broadcast that night, and Brooke Weisbrod was our sideline reporter. The three of us sat courtside as we watched Duke go through their gameday shootaround in an empty KFC Yum Center just about eight hours prior to game time. That shootaround time is crucial to any broadcaster. Not only are we getting our eyes on players in person, but we also are gathering all the information we can about players, coaches, storylines, and points of emphasis being discussed and executed. For me that one-hour gameday practice is the most important part of my preparation. If I listen and watch closely, the game within the game will be revealed. Keys to victory will be emphasized, and the vibe and focus of individual players and team will be obvious.

About halfway through the Duke practice that day, head coach Mike Krzyzewski made his way over to the end of the scorers' table where Rece and I were taking notes as we observed the Blue Devils in their preparation. You never really know how much time you will get or how revealing a head coach is going to be with you on the day of a game, so we listened intently as Coach Krzyzewski talked about his team, the possible effects of having just won on the road against the No. 3 ranked team in the nation (Virginia) just three days earlier, and his concerns with Louisville and the challenge they would pose.

When a head coach visits with you on the day of a game, you listen with a purpose. When the winningest coach in the history of men's division basketball is speaking, you take notes, you learn, and you listen intently.

Coach K, as he is commonly referred to, is a Hall of Fame coach who has led the Duke program to five national championships and 12 Final Four appearances, heading into the 2019–20 season. He has won six gold medals as the head coach of U.S. men's national teams and produced more lottery picks and won more NCAA Tournament games than any coach in the history of the game. Under his leadership Duke has become a dynasty that few programs in any sport can match. Uncommon winning by any definition of the term—that sums up the career of Mike Krzyzewski.

As Coach K kept one eye keenly aware of his players during our conversation, he began to talk about the importance of being a leader and what that looks like in his mind. A graduate of the U.S. Military Academy, it's a topic he excels in, having left the United States Army in 1974 after obtaining the rank of captain. I was caught off guard and surprised when he shared with Rece and me that there are times as a head coach during a game that he simply does not know what to do, what changes to make, or what to tell his team. That's powerful insight and authentic talk from the all-time winningest coach in the history of the game. I asked him directly, "What do you do when those times come?"

His response was straightforward and thought provoking. "I never let my actions or words display that I am not confident in what we are going to do next," he said. "You have to have a strong face even if you don't feel strong. Reflecting back to my time in the military, your men better not see any hesitation or uncertainty. The leader has to display total confidence at all times. I guard my words and only speak positive things until I am certain of the direction we need to go. You can speak it into action if you do."

I jotted down that response, so I could refer to it during the course of the game that night. Little did I know how prophetic that statement would be less than nine hours later in that same arena. From the opening tip, Duke was dominated by Louisville. Everything in that game was in favor of the home team. Louisville carved up the Duke half-court man-to-man defense, played a suffocating pack-line defense, and frustrated the visitors at every turn. The Yum Center was roaring as Louisville took an 11-point lead into the halftime locker room. The No. 2-ranked team in the country was on the ropes. Louisville had not only made Duke face a deficit, but the Cardinals also had done it by giving more effort and outcompeting a young Duke team in the first 20 minutes. Something had to change or Duke was headed back to Durham, North Carolina, with just their second loss of the 2019 ACC regular season.

Something did change to start the second half. Duke made just two of their first 17 shots to start the second half, and the lead grew to 23 points for Louisville with just more than nine minutes to play. The ESPN probability factor at that point in the game for a Duke win was 0.1 percent. Basically, this game was over, but it wasn't over.

Coach K switched defenses to a 2-2-1 three-quarter-court press. Louisville settled for a couple of bad, quick shots, and suddenly a little bit of life was beginning to develop on that Duke sideline. The press that Coach K switched to was working, and Louisville began to panic. Turnovers and empty possessions by Louisville on offense opened the door, but was there enough time to pull it off? The numbers said no. The voice in the Duke huddle said yes.

A Duke team that had been thoroughly outplayed in every area of basketball caught fire. And over the last 9:30 minutes of the game, Duke was spectacular. A 23-point lead by Louisville was suddenly a tie game when Duke freshman Cam Reddish nailed a three-point shot with 1:14 to play. He followed that shot up with two made free throws with 14 seconds to play, giving Duke a two-point lead, and when the final horn went off, Duke had won the game 71–69. In doing so, the Blue Devils secured the biggest second-half comeback in Coach K's history at Duke. A 35–10 run by Duke to close out the game was extraordinary to watch. The Yum Center was stunned, as the unimaginable had just occurred.

Brooke was quickly in position to interview Duke freshman sensation Zion Williamson within a minute after the final horn. The future No. 1 overall pick in the 2019 NBA Draft had played through foul trouble down the stretch and finished with 27 points and 12 rebounds. His response to Brooke about what the timeouts were like and what the message was from Coach K in those timeouts was clear, concise, and compelling. "He said he doesn't coach losers; he only coaches winners. 'Go out there and play hard.' He can coach us to a win," Williamson said. "Coach K always told us if we need confidence, look at him."

During his postgame interview, Coach K said he kept telling his guys, "You aren't losers, but you are playing like losers. We are going to win." Even when they were down by 20 points midway through the second half, he kept telling his players they were going to win, though he was not sure he believed it himself. "I did think we could play better. I was hoping we would not lose by 35," Coach K said. "I'm not kidding. We could have. So you are talking positive, but I don't believe it. Once that press was going, I said, 'We've got a chance here. We can get it.' But at that point, I think I may have been telling them a lie."

Pause for a moment and reflect on what there is to learn from that day on February 12, 2019. Let's start with the obvious. If you were Louisville that night, know how to handle a 2-2-1 press and how to put a game away when you are up 23 with just more than nine minutes to go. Value the ball. Do not take quick, bad shots. Playing not to lose and with fear will get you beat. If you are Duke, you cannot get outworked, outcompeted, and have a deficit in the effort plays if you expect to win. Secondly, good teams find a way to win. The challenge is never too big.

Late that night back in my hotel room, I reflected on that game and kept going back to the conversation Rece and I had with Coach K during the Duke gameday practice. It was like he knew it was coming. His words had come full circle in a period of about 11 hours. "You have to have a strong face even if you don't feel strong," he had said. "You can speak it into action if you do."

I was once again reminded of the power of our spoken words, and my thoughts had very little to do with how to mount a 23-point comeback on the road in the second half. The power of our spoken words can change a game, alter a life, and impact our destiny. As it says in Proverbs 13:3: "He who guards his lips, guards his life. But he, who speaks rashly, will come to ruin."

I have yet to come across too many other scriptures in the Bible more clear-cut than Proverbs 13:3. I have also not found too many other scriptures in the Bible that I personally struggle with more than this one. This part of my own game film is hard for me to watch. If I were to grade my film just on the past week, month, or year of my life, I'm sure I would be ashamed and embarrassed for much of that film. I once heard that it's of great value to get alone and have an honest conversation with your heart. When I take the time to do this, the majority of that conversation between me and my heart centers on the words I use and how I say them.

Bob Knight won three national titles as the head basketball coach at Indiana University and coached the United States Olympic team to a gold medal at the 1984 Summer Olympics in Los Angeles, California. You could argue that he and Krzyzewski have impacted the game of basketball as much as any other coaching duo you can find. Regardless of whether or not you agree or even have an opinion on Coach Knight's style of coaching, the fact remains he is a Hall of Fame coach who had great success throughout his career. "You cannot win before you eliminate losing," he said.

I believe that to be a true statement. And if I am ever going to win at the level I desire to win in my life as a husband, dad, and a man after God's own heart, I must eliminate the lack of discipline I have at times with my own spoken words. I will not win like I want to win or consistently show others how an authentic God can change your life until I first eliminate what causes me to lose. And more times than not, it's my tongue.

As a college basketball analyst for ESPN, I have a responsibility to speak words that are accurate every time I put on a headset or clip on a microphone to broadcast a college basketball game on national television. I must give opinions that are formed through knowledge and preparation. I should speak words that are informative and, as an analyst, tell why specific things are happening in the game. I am an analyst therefore I should not be talking about *what* just happened. People watching the game on their television or online can see *what* just happened. My job and the job of any analyst is to tell *why* something just took place. At times I should be entertaining and on other occasions I have to be critical. All of this has to be done within the guidelines for those who work for a major TV network like ESPN. Like most others who work in this profession, I do not take this responsibility lightly. Psalm 141:3 says: "Set a guard over my mouth, Lord. Keep watch over the door of my lips."

Over the years I have learned the value of praying about the words I will speak during each broadcast. I want protection over my spoken words I use on my job. Critical ears are listening and waiting to pounce at any mistake or inaccuracy that I may say. I know that my words will not always please everyone who is listening, but my heart desires for God's protection to be over me as I speak. I pray for boldness to do my job with excellence and insight. I ask God to protect me from speaking words that would be hurtful or harmful to anyone, including myself.

The career that God has provided me with at this time in my life is very important to me and my family. I desire God's hand of favor to be upon me as I work. I very much want His blessings. Like the majority of you reading this book, my career is important to me, so I pray about my words before I ever arrive at those arenas on gameday. The last thing I do before leaving my hotel room before any game or studio assignment is kneel and spend time with God.

I have developed a high priority with the words I use while doing my job. It's evident by my prayers asking God to protect me and give me favor in this area of my life. I am intentional about the spoken words I use and am disciplined in this pursuit. My spoken words are of tremendous value to me in my work life. Unfortunately, my spoken words in every other area of my life are not viewed with that same priority. My day-to-day conversations and interactions with others is inconsistent, careless, and at times hurtful to myself and others. The value I place on my professional words has not carried over to other areas of my life.

So why have I missed the importance of this when it comes to the words I speak every day? Why do I place far more emphasis on the words I use on ESPN than I do with my own wife, daughter, and those I interact with on a daily basis? I have far less discipline with my tongue when I'm not wearing a headset sitting courtside than I do the other 22 hours of any given day. As I look at my film in this area, it's clear to me something needs to change. For the most part, I am getting my butt kicked on a daily basis in this area of my life. Again, if

I'm going to win, I must first eliminate losing, and more times than not, it's a lack of discipline with my tongue that trips me up the most.

God's written word is full of warnings and lessons about the power of our spoken words, the harm they can cause us, and the good our spoken words can bring to ourselves and others if we control what we say and how we say it. Sometimes the way we say something is more important than what you are actually saying. Colossians 4:6 reads: "Let your conversation be always full of grace, seasoned with salt, so that you may know how to answer everyone."

When I listen to my game film from time to time, close my eyes, and turn up the volume, I am not always proud of what I hear. My words are not full of grace or seasoned with salt as God instructs in Colossians 4:6. I hear a tone at times with my wife, our daughter, and those closest to me that can be harsh, hurtful, and sharp. I am reminded that how you speak to your children becomes their inner voice, and it's one of the most important things a parent should understand.

As a dad the impact of my words is heavier than the words of anyone else in my daughter's life. No one can tear her down or build her up quicker than I. Your children are no different than mine. The words we use as a dad and the tone we say them with are not equally weighted with everyone else in our children's lives. Nor should they be. As the designed leader of our home, our words should have the most impact. The question becomes: what impact are your words truly having?

I'm fine with laying it all out there right now and being transparent with you on this. If I do a thorough job of evaluating my film in this area, I know what I am going to find. I will hear quick responses to people that can be harsh, critical, and judgmental. I speak words about other people that are sometimes spoken out of jealousy, pride, anger, and insecurity. I hear curse words every now and then that I absolutely would not accept from that boy who wants to date my daughter someday, but she hears them from me on occasion. I hear words that are simply not true and do not align with what God says about me in His written word.

I want to pause here for a moment and look at what God says about who I am and who you are. Maybe very few people out there have the same struggle I do in this area. I just know when I really evaluate the words I use on a day-to-day basis that they do not always match up with what God has promised to those who believe in Him. In 2 Timothy 1:7, it says: "For God did not give us a spirit of timidity, but a spirit of power, of love, and of self-discipline."

That is a very simple promise from God, but I find myself at times saying words that are not in agreement with this verse at all. I do speak words of fear about a situation I am facing. I say words that do not show love and compassion for others, and my lack of self-discipline with my tongue has hurt me on numerous occasions. I wonder how my situation would change if the next time I became fearful and worried about something that I would literally say out loud the words of 2 Timothy 1:7 and speak it into action instead of verbalizing my fearful thoughts and concerns.

I am wanting all of us to open our hearts and our minds to our spoken words in a new and fresh way. God is for us, not against us. He desires an abundant life for us, and I believe the discipline of our tongues plays a much bigger role in those blessings than we realize. Like many of you, I have been a part of Bible studies and accountability groups over the years. In one of those early morning Bible studies I was attending in the fall of 2017, the topic was taming our tongues, focusing on the book of James chapter 3. That part of the New Testament is so clear and concise about allowing the Holy Spirit to give us more power to monitor and control what we say.

The question was asked that particular morning for a real-life example of someone guarding their words and the impact it had. One of my neighbors, Craig Lile, quickly stood up and stated to the group that he had an example from his days as a professional golfer that had left an imprint on his own heart about controlling one's tongue and how it can change the trajectory of our paths.

Craig played collegiate golf at the University of Arkansas from 1997 to 2001. He was a two-time All-American for the Razorbacks and racked up five individual titles his senior year. He turned pro right out of college and played in the South African Sunshine Tour from 2002 to 2008, the Nationwide Tour in the United States from 2003 to 2011, and the PGA Tour in 2007.

On a side note, Craig is one heck of a nice guy and the best golfer in our neighborhood. I personally love golf, and any professional golf story told by a guy with a South African accent is easy for me to listen to.

The room was silent as Craig began his story. "About 10 years ago, I was partnered with Justin Rose on the final day of the Alfred Dunhill Championship at the Houghton Golf Club in Johannesburg, South Africa," he said. "I remember being excited to play that round in particular because it was my first time to ever play with Justin. He was young in his career but had a ton of hype and promise about his game, having finished tied for fourth in the 1998 British Open as an amateur after a dramatic birdie on the 18th hole in the final round. Justin turned pro the next day after that 1998 top five finish in the Open Championship and was ranked inside the top 50 in the world as we stepped to the first tee. I was thrilled to be competing against one of the top golfers in the world. For the next five hours, however, Justin Rose was anything but a top 50 golfer. He hit it right, he hit it left, he hit it in the water, and over houses out of bounds into places you thought would be impossible to hit it. It was confusing at times and hard to watch. But even more confusing to me were the words Justin used throughout the entire round.

"Every poor shot and every bad swing was followed by positive words from Justin to his caddy—phrases like, 'Man, that was so close.' 'I am almost there.' 'Just missed perfect on that one.' 'It's starting to come around. I can feel it.' 'Next swing will be pure.' But nothing about how he was playing backed those words up. I remember at one point turning to my own caddy and saying this guy has lost it. How in the world is he a top 50 player on tour? And why does he continue to talk to himself after every missed hit?"

And then Craig made a statement that I had never heard before. "Justin Rose encouraged himself and spoke positives about himself better than I have ever heard another person building up another person," he said.

That line was awesome. We have all heard phenomenal motivational talks from one person to another or from one person to an entire team or speeches that are 100 percent positive and reinforcing. Those talks feed and fuel confidence to a performance. But I have never heard an example of a person talking to themselves with that type of passion or persistence, especially in the middle of the action.

Craig said he shook Rose's hand at the end of the round, wished him good luck down the road, and told him it was a pleasure to play with him. But walking away from that handshake, he was thinking, *What did I just see for the past four hours, and how in the world is Rose gonna last on the pro tour?*

But the very next weekend—after playing a round of golf like I play on my home course in Arkansas—Rose found himself in a playoff for the title on the final day of a PGA event back in the United States. Craig stated that he turned on the TV that following weekend and was shocked to see the same guy, who was brutal just a week earlier, was in position to win a tournament. "And my thoughts raced quickly back to the round we had played just six days earlier. All I could think about was the lack of control he had that day with his driver and irons, but the perfect control he maintained over his tongue," Craig said. "I knew I had just witnessed a very important lesson for my own life. Justin Rose had spoken it into action, and I saw the payoff that resulted from it."

If you are not familiar with professional golf or Justin, just realize this. That same golfer who struggled for 18 holes with Craig has gone on to an amazing career. After missing the cut in the first 21 pro events he played early in his career, Rose has now won more than 20 combined championships between the PGA and European Tour. He won his first major tournament in 2013 by finishing first in the U.S. Open. He won a gold medal in the men's individual tournament in the

2016 Summer Olympics in Rio de Janeiro. Rose was the No. 1-ranked player in the world during the 2018 season and was the FedEx Cup Playoff champion that same year.

I did not include this story to convince you that your words on the golf course will influence your score. This is not about the power of positive thinking or speaking prosperity into your life. It is, however, another look at how our words are tied directly to our thoughts, our attitudes, our actions, and our outlook on life.

What is your reaction when it appears things are not going your way? Are you quick to spout off negative words of worry, confusion, and anger? Do you speak into action the worst-case scenario you can come up with? How disciplined are you at monitoring your words and controlling what you say when your first reaction is to verbalize your negative thoughts? Are you contradictory with your speech by sometimes speaking words that are truthful and pleasing to God, but in the next breath, your tongue is violent and destructive?

Maybe there's only a few of you that have a similar struggle like I do when watching your film. If that's the case, that's awesome. I hope someday to have that kind of consistent discipline with my tongue. I just know when I really listen to what my game film sounds like, I need to develop an unquenchable desire to get better if improvement is going to occur. I must become more intentional about my spoken words just like I do with my words on my job. So if nothing else, I needed to write and reflect on this part of my film simply for me. I want greater success than I am currently experiencing. But before I can win, I must eliminate losing. Those careless, heavy, and harmful words that are quick to fire out of my mouth must become less, and a tongue that is full of grace and seasoned with salt must become greater.

Your life will move in the direction of your words. When you stop to evaluate that statement, it should get your full attention. My wife, Tiffany, and our daughter, Kennedy, are counting on me to be the tone setter in our home. It's my responsibility as a man to lead our home in word and action. God is very specific to us as men about how we are to speak to our families. Read Colossians 3:19-21 and let those verses seep into your soul.

Do not be harsh with your wife, do not embitter your children. Can you or I ever justify words that are ultimately destroying the heart and hope of those we are responsible to lead? How easy it is to scorch the life of those closest to us with an undisciplined tongue. You and I can burn down our marriage and any shot of a relationship with our children with heated words. I am humbled quickly when I read in the Bible that we all will one day be accountable for every spoken word we have ever said. Jesus spoke very clearly about idle words and the impact they have, but his warning often goes unnoticed or ignored. Jesus said that on the day of judgment we all will be held responsible for every idle word we spoke. As I read that last line, I do expect for Jesus to warn us about profanity, blasphemy, or intentional harsh use of the tongue. But I am caught a little off guard by the idle words warning. Idle words are those words we just spout off carelessly without considering their impact on people and the harm they may be causing to others. It's empty rhetoric or insincere, exaggerated talk. I sense that many people assume that the sins of our tongue are minor in the big picture of sin, and that insincere or exaggerated talk will be overlooked on the day of judgment. That is simply not the case. Jesus spoke specifically about the destruction our tongues can cause. We should all take heed. In Matthew 12:36-37, Jesus said, "But I tell you that men will have to give account on the day of judgment for every careless word they have spoken. For by your words, you will be acquitted, and by your words, you will be condemned."

I am far from where I need to be in this area of my life. But I can promise you, nothing has my attention any more these days than this. I am responsible for what I say and how I am saying it, and one day I will give an account for my performance.

Like any dad who has a daughter, I want the absolute best for Kennedy in her life. I have prayed for her future husband since the time she was born. I know the type of guy I desire for her to marry someday. But here is where the rubber meets the road. Kennedy is going to search for those same qualities in her future husband, as she has seen in me while growing up in our home. How I speak to and treat Tiffany is exactly what she will be attracted to in her husband one day. It happens all of the time. Girls are forming what they will search for in their husbands by watching and listening to how their dad communicates and treats their mom. How about that for something to mull over? If you remember nothing else about this book, remember that statement. If I remember nothing else about writing this book, I hope I remember it as well.

Please let this sink in. Don't just read it and move on. What does your game film look like on this play? What are you saying and how are you saying it? There is no place more important than our own homes when it comes to the words we speak, the tone we say them with, and how they align with God's written word. Just fast forward your film to that spot. What do you sound like in your home?

It blows my mind how parents are speaking to each other, to officials, to coaches, their own kids, and other kids these days. No curse word is off limits. Demeaning, derogatory, foolish words are spewed out from overly opinionated people. It goes on from the youngest of pee-wee games to high school and college sports. I am as competitive as anyone out there. I understand the desire to see your child have success. I know the frustration that comes with the umpiring in Little League ball or the officiating in summer travel basketball. I have felt the disappointment when your kid doesn't get to play as much as you think he or she should. But guess what? It's not about me and it's not about you. The success or lack of success our children have in sports is not an indication of how good of a parent we are. But having a child who is respectful of authority, disciplined with their own tongue, gives great effort, and is coachable, tough, and a caring teammate *is* a direct reflection of how we are doing as a mom and dad. Society as a whole has this *completely* out of balance. Kentucky coach John Calipari has a great point when recruiting a player. "If I walk in a home and a kid disrespects a woman, his mother, or grandmother, then I am out," he said. "I won't recruit them."

I have seen kids at every level lose the love they have for something because of how their parents spoke and acted during and after their competition. I am all for teaching kids how to compete, work, push through adversity, and develop a will to fight and to win. Like many of you, I have zero tolerance for lack of effort and I have no use for participation ribbons and trophies that seem to get passed out like candy at every youth game these days. That's not how the real world works. I get it. I am living it. I understand how a parent wants their kid to succeed more than anything. But I also know how easy it is to get things out of balance in life, and nowhere is it more difficult to keep a proper perspective than how you handle your child through Little League baseball, high school football, youth soccer, or dance competitions. Don't get mad at me right now if this is making you a little uncomfortable. Watch your game film and listen closely. You will hear what you need to hear.

Look at your film with a keen eye and listen to it with open ears. Reflect back on some of the recent conversations you have had with your son or daughter on the drive home from a game, competition, or match. What did you say about other parents on the team? Ask yourself how other parents are talking about you on their drive home. What words did you use when talking about the coach, other kids on your team, or the officials and umpires? What did you speak into the heart of your very own child about his or her performance?

We may not listen with our hearts as adults, but our children listen with their hearts, especially when it comes from Mom or Dad. This is a huge responsibility that many are missing the mark on. Proverbs 21:23 says: "He who guards his mouth and his tongue keeps himself from calamity."

The importance of disciplining our tongues is not a new concept. Look at the story of Joshua and how his army overtook the city of Jericho. I find it interesting that during those seven days that Joshua's army marched around the walls of Jericho that Joshua instructed his men to not say a single word until the day he told them to shout.

God knows the power of spoken words as well as the power of unspoken words. I believe God laid it on Joshua's heart to demand silence as they marched those seven days for a reason. Had Joshua not given them the instruction to keep quiet, I am pretty certain after about one lap on Day One that somebody marching would have started complaining and questioned this crazy plan they were executing to bring down the walls of Jericho. And one person would have become two, two would have multiplied to four, and quickly, the power of spoken words would have derailed the plan that God had given them.

We do not have to say every thought that comes into our minds. Pray and ask God for discipline in this area of your life. Remember that lesson we all learned in kindergarten: "If you can't say something nice about someone, don't say anything at all." That is so simple and so true and for the most part so forgotten, and it applies to words you say about yourself just as much as words you say about others. Determine that you are no longer going to give the enemy an open door to destruction in your life in this area. Decide to be excellent at these two things: guarding your thoughts when you are alone by yourself and guarding your words when you are with other people. If you make progress in those two areas, the trajectory of your life will certainly change.

I am completely on board with all of those lessons we want our kids to learn through sports. I cannot stand laziness, selfishness, lack of fight, and lack of toughness. I know how competitive youth sports are these days. I understand the financial blessing a college scholarship can be, but I want to remind you that God's word does not change just because selection to a youth All-Star travel team, the front line on the cheerleading squad, or a potential college scholarship is on the line. We will all give an account for our every spoken word someday. I fail in this area as much as anyone, but my word choice has my attention and a greater priority in my life these days.

I challenge you to spend time each morning talking with God about the words you will choose to use each day. Ask for His protection so your words are not hurtful or harmful to anyone, including yourself. Begin speaking words that add victory into your life, not defeat. We already have enough junk that is against us and trying to hold us back. You will never be perfect in what you say and how you say it. The tongue battle is constant. You and I are never safe. We will never arrive at perfection. No man can control his tongue in all ways at all times. The Bible is crystal clear about that. But there is an accountability factor for all of us that we will one day answer for.

It won't just happen overnight, but small steps of progress can be made immediately if it's important to you. It boils down to a constant submission to God. Surrender your words daily to Him. Ask early each morning for His Holy Spirit to help you. Surrender your tongue to His will, confess with your tongue when you fail, ask forgiveness immediately when it is needed, and charge on. Make this a daily practice. Success will be found.

Remember: "He who guards his lips, guards his life. But he who speaks rashly will come to ruin." What a promise from God. The impact of our words is once again driven home. The promise from God doesn't say guards "his job, his money, or his stuff." It simply says guards "his life." What a promise. What a challenge. How foolish it would be to ignore.

Perhaps no area is more important than what we are saying and how we are saying it. Psalm 19:14 says: "May the words of my mouth and the meditation of my heart be pleasing in your sight, O Lord, my rock and my redeemer."

As you listen to your game film right now, what do you hear? Ask God to help you in this crucial area. When we are growing as believers, we should allow the Holy Spirit to take control over more areas of our lives. You cannot emphasize everything at once. If you do, nothing will get accomplished. Pick one or two key areas at a time and focus your attention on those things. Your words and how you say them should have high priority.

Chapter 4

FORGIVENESS

Hate. It has caused a lot of problems in this world, but it has not solved one yet.

—MAYA ANGELOU

I N THE WORLD of television and sports broadcasting, the word talent refers to the announcers and reporters who call the action and describe the game. The talent is on camera, and their voices are providing facts, insight, perspective, and opinions to the viewers watching at home. I am not certain when or how the announcers on a game were first labeled as the talent on a broadcast, but those of us who work for ESPN on camera would all agree that the off-camera folks are supremely talented in what they do and truly are the heart and soul of any production team. Producers, directors, associate producers, associate directors, camera and replay operators, graphics operators, and audio technicians all make up the core of the technical crew for each broadcast. No matter how "talented" the announcers are (or think we are), we are not even getting on the air without a truly talented technical crew grinding away behind the scenes. Every successful broadcast is a total team effort by everyone involved. The talent and the technical crew all do their jobs with passion, purpose, and skill. I marvel at the skill of the individuals on the production crew at ESPN. And when folks from the technical crew and talent side all come together for a seminar or brainstorming session at our home campus in Bristol, Connecticut, the entire room is full of talent in my eyes. I know firsthand how good those folks are at what they do.

I have been going to talent seminars for more than 20 years at ESPN. It is pretty much an annual occurrence. Sometimes it's sport specific, and sometimes it's not. These meetings are held a majority of the time at our Bristol campus and serve to set the tone, cast a vision, and build team concepts for the upcoming season or year. These meetings that normally last a couple of days are of great value in connecting the entire ESPN production team.

In late summer of 2008, I was in Bristol to attend the College Football Seminar in preparation for the upcoming season. I was working at the time as both a college basketball analyst and college football sideline reporter for ESPN. After dinner on the first day, several of us in attendance got together for a short Bible study and to share about our faith and the challenges that come with being on the road for work, the pressures of the job, and how it all should fit in with our walk with God. Guys like Kirk Herbstreit, Todd Blackledge, Dave Pasch, and Chris Spielman challenged me that night, just hearing where they were in pursuit of knowing God in a deeper way. We wanted to stay connected and encourage one another throughout the year. I volunteered to send out a short email devotional on a weekly basis just as a reminder to keep our eyes lifted up to our Heavenly Father as we managed the chaos of a college football season.

"The Huddle" was the name I attached to the group email that was sent out that season, and over the course of a four-year period, that original email list of eight guys grew to nearly 1,000 as high school, college, and professional coaches were added to the list, along with many others in the broadcasting industry. The list of names on "The Huddle" was far more impressive than any devotional challenge I ever sent them, but it was cool to watch God grow that list and challenge men and women to a fresh, authentic walk with Him.

As I was looking back through some of those original emails from 2008 to 2009, I came across one of "The Huddle" devotionals that I had sent out. It was a brief, two-paragraph challenge about forgiveness, the importance of forgiving those who offend you, and the impact that it has on our journey with God. Reading that email from more than 10 years ago, I realized my understanding of forgiveness back then was at a very basic level. I had a grasp on the forgiveness of sins that is offered through Jesus and putting trust in him dying on the cross. I understood my entire relationship with Him is based on that one word—forgiveness. But I was at the crawling stage of forgiveness in terms of putting the words I had written in that email into action. My dad is 84 years old. He always said, "A person thinks they are really fast—until they actually race against someone who is really fast. Then you find out who you are."

That same common sense statement about racing equates to forgiveness. You may think you know all you need to know about forgiveness until it's your turn to forgive. And at the time of that writing back in 2008, I thought I knew all I needed to know about that word, forgiveness. Man, was I wrong, and God took me to task over it.

I have seen God work in my life in different areas, in different ways, and with different time frames. Some lessons are quicker than others, some are more taxing than others, and some are of greater impact than others. And for me forgiveness was extremely long, extremely difficult, and extremely humbling. Those two paragraphs I wrote back in 2008 on forgiveness were words of knowledge I had in my mind about the topic. The words I write today are from my heart, a heart touched by a gracious, loving God, who is very serious about forgiveness.

God began speaking to me about forgiveness, resentment, and animosity I was holding in my heart toward others in a very soft way during my early morning time with Him in the summer of 2012. I was not searching for this lesson. I was simply sitting on a rock on the shores of Lake Estes in Estes Park, Colorado, reading through my morning devotional book, when the word forgiveness grabbed my attention and grabbed my heart like never before. I knew that God was speaking directly to me that morning from the pages of that book. And that's when the journey began.

At first, I didn't want to hear, acknowledge, or respond to what God was speaking to me about in this area of my life. I tried to ignore His voice and brush off His nudge, but time and time again, I found myself going back to those few pages on forgiveness and wrestling with it. Initially, I was too busy and too prideful to listen. That is a bad combination. But God is persistent and God is relentless. When He wants to teach us something, He is going to do it, and God was dragging me straight to His class on a cleansed heart when it comes to forgiving others. How long it takes to learn the lesson is often determined by how teachable we are. But regardless of our stubbornness, He will not change His purpose. God loves us too much to allow us to plateau and remain stagnant in crucial areas of life. In the summer of 2012, I was absolutely stuck while refusing to let go of the two-hand grip I had on unforgiveness toward others.

God pursued me with a specific purpose, as He often times will. And after hours of time alone with Him, becoming purposeful in my submission to His word, and eventually asking for a changed heart in this area of my life, God did just that.

Read slowly what I am about to tell you. *No other act is tied to obedience more than the act of forgiveness.* I can still show you the exact rock I was sitting on at Lake Estes over a decade ago when God first laid that statement on my heart. Up until that morning, I had never considered that forgiveness was a form of obedience, and that having a heart full of resentment, bitterness, and hard feelings toward others was creating a wall between me and God.

I had zero desire to go to a new level of forgiveness prior to that time in my life. I tried to run from what God was speaking to me, but we cannot outrun a relentless God. He began showing me that forgiveness wasn't about what I thought I deserved, the excuses I had, or the level of anger someone or some circumstance had deposited into my life. Forgiveness is secured by obedience to His word, and I was clearly insecure in this area of my heart.

I have never been to seminary or taken courses on theology. My understanding of the Bible is likely limited compared to many of you reading this book right now. But I do remember studying the sixth chapter of Matthew during several of those early morning quiet times in the months following that vacation day in Colorado. After reading Matthew 6, verses 14–15, it was distinct and somewhat startling to me how God viewed forgiveness. It says: "For if you forgive men when they sin against you, your Heavenly Father will also forgive you. But if you do not forgive men of their sins against you, your Father will not forgive your sins."

That's it. Two sentences that did not leave a lot of room for interpretation. And as I absorbed that verse over a two-to-three-week period, I simplified it down to two questions. Do I believe this verse to be true, and if so, what was I going to do about it?

The first answer was easy. Of course, I believed it to be true. I am not one to question God's written word. But the second question was not and still is not as effortless or painless. What was I going to do about it? That began simmering in my heart.

It didn't take me long to come to this realization. When we choose not to forgive, we are denying our common ground as sinners in need of God's forgiveness. I know a few things to be true in my life. One of those truths is that I am going to fail and come up short every single day one way or another. It may be through my choice of words. It may be an attitude or thought that I carry around with me. It may be how I treat someone, gossip about others, pride, lust, etc. I sin in my life every day just like you do. And I know I need forgiveness of my sin just like you do.

So I was at a crossroad. At least, that is how I felt. I was either going to trust God's word and allow it to change my life or I was going to continue in my prideful, arrogant ways and cling to bitterness and resentment. It was very clear that I had an issue, and if I did not deal with it, I was going to face the consequences of having unforgiveness inside my heart.

God began patiently showing me that true forgiveness is based on a daily choice to live my life grounded on grace and love for others. I was so far off base on this one that I wasn't even in the game. Over the course of my life, I had developed a fighting mentality. I kept score with people in a lot of ways. If you hurt me, I was going to somehow get even. If you spoke negatively about me, I was going to speak negatively about you. If you did me wrong, I was going to hope it came back on you in return. I kept score and I wanted to win. By the world's standards, this approach was normal. By selfish, prideful, arrogant ways, this was acceptable. But as we all know, God's ways are different than the world's ways, and He began calling me to a new destination in relation to forgiveness.

When you live your life with a keeping score mentality, no one wins. I can guarantee you one thing: in any relationship both you and the other person are at some point not going to see eye to eye. You will disagree, make mistakes, say hurtful words, and disappoint the other person. It does not matter who you are or how long that relationship has been occurring. Somewhere along the line, something is going to be said, or something is going to be done that requires forgiveness.

When an offense occurs, if that relationship is going to endure and move forward, you have to have a heart that is ruled by forgiveness instead of blame. When God first began adjusting my heart regarding forgiveness, it wasn't just about me forgiving people who had offended me at some point in my life. What my eyes were actually opened to was that *any* unforgiveness in my heart is sin. You cannot be intimate with God while holding hands with sin. Unforgiveness separates us from God, and being separate from God is a dangerous place to be.

I have learned a few things about forgiveness in recent years. If you wait to forgive until you feel like forgiving, chances are that it will never happen. Pride and time have a way of convincing us it's okay to just move on. Don't be deceived like I was for many years. Moving on is not forgiveness.

I believe true forgiveness, the kind of self-yielding forgiveness that God calls us to, can only come by exhaustively purifying your heart toward another person or situation. You confess that you are no different than the person who offended you. You are a real person with real faults, standing on common ground in desperate need of God's forgiveness in your life. You must then be extremely intentional about asking God to cleanse your heart of bitterness, resentment, or hatred toward that person or situation. I love these synonyms for the word cleanse. Ask God to disinfect, sanitize, launder, purify, scour, and scrub your heart of bitterness, resentment, and hatred.

Forgiving others is serious business. I have seen the damage that is caused by not completely finishing off the process and allowing just the slightest amount of resentment and bitterness toward someone to remain in your heart. I believe God knows that complete forgiveness never comes naturally to someone. We just are not wired with that type of heart. So to make certain the job was complete, God added a final closing chapter, one more lap to run, and one more obstacle to clear. Romans 12:14 says: "Bless those who persecute you; bless and do not curse them."

Bless those who persecute you? Ask for favor from God upon those who have hurt me? You have got to be kidding me. Well, God is serious about forgiveness, but obedient, self-yielding forgiveness takes place when you begin praying specifically for God to bless that person or situation you have been offended by. Read that again.

I cannot tell you that I am 100 percent in on wanting God to bless those who have presecuted me, disappointed me, or inflicted some type of hurt into my life. I hope someday I will truly have a consistent heart in this area. I have made great strides and progress in this area since the morning this whole forgiveness lesson began for me in Colorado. I have felt God melt away resentment, animosity, and bitterness I had toward others but only when I disciplined myself to pray for God to bless those who have hurt me.

I understand why God instructs us in the book of Romans to pray with this type of purpose in our life. He is our creator and He knows exactly who we are and how we are wired. If we can hold onto just a sliver of resentment, we are darn sure going to do it. At least I am. I may forgive you in my mind and heart to the best of my ability, but I will stop at that point and consider the forgiveness job completed. But stopping at that point is like walking off the job early. Those roots of hard feelings, anger, and resentment will grow like wild weeds if the entire root is not removed. God demands a pure heart—not an almost pure heart.

So it goes back to a choice that we must make. Will you choose to be obedient in praying for those who have offended you or will you not? It is a choice that requires a humble spirit, an intense heart for God, and an uncommon obedience. I encourage you to memorize Romans 12:14 and let it settle into the depths of your soul. The word blessed is defined as "to invoke divine favor upon." Only a clear heart can ask for that type of favor.

God is serious about forgiveness and God is serious about showing grace to others. This level of grace seems extreme to you and me, but I believe God knows the danger of harboring *any* part of unforgiveness in our lives. Consistent prayers of blessing for another person will sweep away those last remaining pieces of anger and bitterness.

Many of you have gone through situations that have caused feelings of agony and pain I can't even imagine. Hardship may have lasting effects because of something that someone has done. I will never understand how you feel. No one may ever truly understand the sorrow and suffering that you have endured. Forgiveness of that situation may seem impossible to you. I can only encourage you to fall on the side of obedience as God speaks to your heart.

Our Heavenly Father knows everything about us. He understands that when you first begin praying for those who have offended you that you may very well be praying strictly out of obedience toward what He has called you to do. That's understandable for a period of time. God is persistent at times, but He is also patient. Keep your heart approachable toward God. Allow Him time to do His work in your heart. Patience and no shortcuts will yield results. You will eventually find that it is impossible to consistently ask God to bless a person in ways that only He can do and still hold onto resentment toward that person. Time, obedience, and unwavering faith in what God can do will eventually rinse your heart of the baggage you have tightly held onto. Your timeline for this heart cleansing process may look completely different than others. You may at some point feel as if you have reached a point of exhaustion in the chase to cleanse your heart. The question is: will you quit or will you keep pursuing?

I'm not sure showing true forgiveness is more important anywhere than in our homes. If your family looks anything similar to mine, you may have several opportunities a day to make a choice. Are you going to be a family that operates out of love and grace for each other or are you going to hold grudges, live in stretches of silence and bitterness, and ultimately allow the enemy an opened door into your home?

Unforgiveness in our hearts separates us from God. Unforgiveness in our home separates us from each other. I believe the most important quality a home can have is forgiveness. I say that because we all have a way of offending those we love. I can be disrespectful, graceless, or short with my wife or daughter much quicker than any other person that may cross my path in a single day. Maybe you aren't like that; I just know that's how I am. And if I don't take the lead in asking for forgiveness, I am not leading my home the way a dad and husband is called to do. Certainly, the goal should be to never snap back or have harsh words with one another. I just don't know how realistic that is. What is realistic, however, is a home that forgives quickly, selflessly, and generously.

I cannot tell you the number of times early on in our marriage that I did not handle disagreements and arguments the proper way. I was content going to sleep at night angry, prideful, and determined to win, not give in. Shutting Tiffany out of my life for a brief period of time was my choice and my decision on how to deal with conflict. I was okay with the silence in our home for hours at a time after an argument or disagreement. I was a fool.

Those hours or days of holding grudges, allowing anger to seep into your heart, and putting a wall up between you and your spouse are prime times for the enemy to attack. Remember he's watching your film. He zooms in on those times of silence and separation that we choose to have. Do all you can to minimize those moments. Know the damage that is being caused. Choose obedience when obedience is hard to choose.

The last thing to grade on your film when looking at forgiveness is whether there's a delay in your forgiveness right now. Has God spoken to you and revealed to you on film a person, a situation, or a hurt that you know is contaminating your soul and stealing life from your body, but you continue to ignore God's voice and remain unmoved by His nudge? Delayed forgiveness is dangerous. Delayed forgiveness is prideful. Delayed forgiveness is disobedient. If God has spoken, He has spoken. That is as simple as I can put it.

I have heard amazing stories of forgiveness over the years that I now realize came about because of that one word: obedience. You may have one of those potential stories right now. But how will your story end? Know that there is a blessing on the other side of obedience. Also note that God is serious about forgiveness.

You may still be thinking, *I'm not budging. I won't, I can't, I'll never be able to or want to forgive that person for what they did to me.* Those are real feelings. I know them well. I have experienced them, too. Where do you begin? How does one go from a hardened, unforgiving heart to a peace-filled gracious, forgiving heart? It starts with one word: willingness. You must have a willingness to forgive that person or that situation. Start by saying heartfelt but honest prayers like, "God, I still feel so hurt and angry by this...but I want to forgive. I want to release this to you. Help me...help me be willing to forgive. Help me start to let go of the hurt and the pain. Help me cancel their debt so we can both be free of this." The process won't happen overnight, but it has to start somewhere, and that somewhere is just a small amount of willingness that God can take and grow into a mountain of grace and absolution.

Obedient, self-yielding forgiveness is a choice. You must decide if you are going to be submissive to God and allow His words to bring change into your life or keep your heart closed off to His calling. I know that may seem harsh or lack understanding toward someone whose life has been devastated by a wrong, but God is God, and we are not. Even when it comes to the most difficult, unfair, heartbreaking situations that can come your way in life, forgiveness is still a command from God—not a suggestion or good idea. At some point your heart must embrace and your tongue must confess, "Father, I submit to your word. I will do what you tell me to do." No act is more tied to obedience than the act of forgiveness.

Chapter 5

SURVIVE THE DROUGHT

All the adversity I've had in my life, all my troubles and obstacles, have strengthened me… You may not realize it when it happens, but a kick in the teeth may be the best thing in the world for you.

—Walt Disney

ASTORY OF BIBLICAL proportions in modern times. These type of stories are not common these days, but they do still exist. And that sums up the story of Austin Hatch. He's a walking miracle with an outlook on life that exceeds anyone I have ever known. Hatch survived two private airplane crashes in the span of eight years. As an 8-year-old little boy in 2003, he lost his mom, Julie; his younger brother, Ian; and his older sister, Lindsay, in a plane crash near Fort Wayne, Indiana. Only he and his dad, who was piloting the aircraft, survived the accident.

Eight years later in June of 2011, the unthinkable happened again. Just nine days after committing to play college basketball at the University of Michigan, the private plane his father was again piloting crashed, killing both his dad, Dr. Stephen Hatch, and stepmother, Kim. Austin, a teenager with a promising future in front of him, was the only survivor of that second crash. By the age of 16, he had survived two separate tragedies that had claimed the lives of five family members.

Arnold Barnett, an MIT statistician, says the odds of surviving a plane crash with one fatality involved is 1 in 3.4 million. Austin Hatch survived two of those crashes with multiple fatalities in both. The odds of surviving those two crashes that Austin lived through is one in 11 quadrillion and 560 trillion. That is a 14-digit number. His story is one of Biblical proportions, but his response to that story is one that should change your life.

I had heard about the tragic events of Hatch's young life on many occasions prior to meeting him for the first time at the 2019 Final Four in Minneapolis. He was in attendance to take part in the Legends of the Hardwood breakfast, honoring his former college coach, John Beilein. From the moment we first shook hands, I knew Austin had an unbreakable spirit about him that few ever obtain. I was blown away by his perseverance and determination to fight his way out of a six-week, medically-induced coma after his second plane crash and become a member of the Michigan Wolverine basketball team for a four-year career on that Ann Arbor campus. "To whom much is given, much is expected," he told me during our conversation that morning in Minneapolis while describing how he viewed his life.

It was obvious to me that God had a special calling for Austin. I have learned a great deal from him over the past year through our connections via texts and phone calls. He is as motivating, encouraging, and inspiring as anyone I have ever known. If you want to learn about true toughness and handling adversity in life, spend time with Austin. You will walk away a changed man. He told me that he has heard his entire life the expression that "time heals all wounds." We have all heard that phrase, but Austin added his touch in a way I have never heard before by saying, "But within that time, we have to do our part."

That is so true and spoken from a guy who has been through it. In all of my conversations with him, I never sensed a "why me" attitude or thought. What I do sense is grit, thankfulness, and perspective. That word grit is an important one to Austin when it comes to dealing with adversity and hard knocks in life. Ask him about those four letters, and he will break it down something like this.

Growth Mind-Set—This views adversity as opportunity. We can find a way to grow from any experience in life. Adversity does not define us; instead adversity can refine us.

Resilience—What happens to us is never as important as how we respond. We are not the product of our circumstances. We are the product of how we choose to respond.

Integrity—In the context of overcoming adversity or working to achieve any goal, this is about following through on our commitments. Integrity is doing what we said we would do, especially when our circumstances change.

Team First—We should always think about the team or others first. We must train ourselves to think *we* before *me*.

Think about this for a second. Here is a guy who has endured the unthinkable two separate times in his life. He came out on the other side with this perspective on how to handle a drought, the hardest seasons of life. Propel forward, stay strong, do the right things, put others first. Highlight that line. Those are simple words of truth from a guy who has stared tragedy twice in the eyes and said, "You will not break me."

I listened to Coach tell the story about a conversation he had with Austin one day. He told John, "You know what, Coach. The way I look at it, I have been so blessed through life. I've only had two really bad days." We should all embrace that kind of response.

It's an extremely short list of folks I have met who can match the challenge, heartbreak, and tragedy that Austin already has faced in his young life. Few of us, if any, will ever be called to walk through a drought-filled desert like Austin was forced to walk through. But understand this: we all will at some point face adversity and difficulties that will knock us back, challenge our faith, and confuse our thoughts. We would all benefit greatly by reflecting back on the response by Austin when those times do come.

He and his wife, Abby, currently live in Ann Arbor, Michigan. Abby works for the Michigan athletic department, and he is employed by the Domino's Pizza corporate office and travels around the country as a motivational speaker. If you are ever fortunate enough to hear him speak, his story will get your attention. How he responded to two tragedies should change your perspective on life—like it has mine. "To whom much is given, much is expected," he has said more than once. It's a true statement from a young man who has lived an unimaginable story and now pursues life with an uncommon response.

Droughts are guaranteed to happen. Maybe you have already been through that life-changing dust storm and possibly more than once. Perhaps you are headed into one right now and don't even see it approaching. But it's coming and will come at a time that doesn't make sense, at a time that is not fair and will make you question God, life, and everything in between. That dry season may last days, weeks, months, or years. How do you survive those harshest times of life? Don't wait until adversity strikes to consider your response. Droughts have a way of confusing our thoughts and shaking our core.

I will be honest with you. This is probably the most difficult chapter to write and possibly the most important one for anyone to absorb. We are all pretty decent when it's going our way. If nothing else, we can fake our joy when the finances, the status, the doctor's reports, and the path of our children are all good. But there is no faking it when that real drought hits, and your life spins out of control.

Those long stretches of nothing can take a mighty toll on us. There are those times when you're crying out to God for answers, direction, and change, but days turn into weeks, and weeks turn into months, and you get no response. That's the kind of drought I'm talking about, and it can come upon us in many different forms. Maybe it's all of those days piling up where you have a strained relationship with your son or daughter. They are not engaged with you as a parent, and you see the effects of poor choices and wrong influences on their lives. It could be that you are battling insignificance in your work, health concerns for you or a loved one, addictions, or a heart that is broken by an unfaithful spouse.

Perhaps you live in a home that puts on a good front in the public eye, but in reality it's a home that's separated, searching, and empty. I know of couples who have for years prayed and cried out to God asking for a child, but still there is silence and no fulfillment of their heart's desire. Your drought could be just an accumulation of stuff. Things just have not gone your way. A drought in life can take many forms. What do you do when the confusion, emptiness, and sorrow just will not let up? It's one of the most important questions we all should be prepared to answer.

I have been through droughts in my life and I have had close friends who have experienced them as well. I do know this. We become vulnerable during those stretches of extreme heat and dry days. The enemy loves to attack when we are weak. He recognizes quickly when we are under physical or emotional stress. He circles us like a hungry lion when we are lonely, tired, lacking purpose, weighing big decisions, or faced with uncertainty. I have also seen the enemy really get after people when they are prospering but prideful, forgetting it is by the grace of God for any goodness in their life. But to me:

the battle goes to another level during those long stretches of desperation, and life no longer makes sense.

I want to be as real as I can with you on this subject. Things have pretty much gone my way most of the time. I have had many good things happen to me over the course of my life, but I also know droughts. I have been through them. I have experienced the heartache, pain, grief, and confusion that comes instantly with the loss of a child during pregnancy. My wife and I have been through it and so have many of you. I will never forget that shadow of darkness that seemed to cover my heart and shade my soul when the doctor told Tiffany and me, "There is no heartbeat." The drought began, and in some ways, it never ends.

I want to pause just for a minute to again say how grateful I am for all of the good things God has given me. It's above and beyond what I could ever ask for or deserve, but I do know a drought and the impact it can have. If you are in some form of desperation in your life, please keep reading. You will get through it. And I hope these next few pages will help and encourage you.

So how do you respond when agony is dominating your day, and grief and despair keep you up at night? What should we do when hopelessness tries to grip our heart and not let go?

There are six key areas to focus on and search your film for if you are currently in a battle. These are lessons I have learned through my own difficulties and what I have learned from others.

CONTROL WHAT
YOU CAN CONTROL

When life has knocked you back and it's hard to stand, you are vulnerable, and becoming purposeful in your response is a must. Temptations accompany trials. You cannot just sit there, hope the drought passes, and be defenseless. You cannot afford to lose more ground or dig a deeper hole. I understand how difficult it can be during extended periods of pain or tribulation to muster up even one ounce of fight, but you have to do it. You must have great conviction in a few key areas. Go back and study your film from the last time you were enduring a trial or test. How did you respond? What were you saying to yourself during that stretch? What you verbalize and speak must be guarded with great caution during the hardest of times. If all you do is relent to your natural response, the only things you will hear are words of discouragement, fear, hopelessness, and defeat. You must claim and speak God's words of truth intentionally and with purpose when under attack. If you memorize just one verse to repeat over and over throughout the day, so be it. Find the verse, speak the verse, and repeat. If not, you will drown in your own spoken words. Control what you can control, and our words are a huge part of that equation.

Those voices you allow in your ear may very well need to be shortened to a list of two or three. Make certain you determine who is saying it and what is being said when hard days are coming at you at a relentless pace. Take charge over both the words you are saying to yourself and what is being said to you. You have no room for error on this when enduring a storm.

DO WHAT'S RIGHT

Sometimes we end up in a very confusing, painful, discouraging place in life for no apparent reason. Life just happens. Other times those long stretches of trial can be traced back to a bad decision. We cannot avoid consequences for our actions. The reason for your drought may never be revealed to you. God is God, and we are not. But you cannot let one mistake multiply and get away from doing what you know are the right things to do in life. We all know what is right and what is wrong. I don't have to break that one down or get into that discussion. It is crucial when things are going against you that you don't compound the issue with wrong choices. One common trait I see in great players is they don't allow one mistake to become two during the course of a game.

When it's not going your way, how you treat others becomes magnified. Get your eyes on others. Some droughts are not fair nor make sense. But that doesn't let you off the hook for losing your discipline or getting outside of God's boundaries for our lives. Have the boldness to stay true to your convictions, no matter what. The odds can quickly get stacked against you during those hardest of days. Obedience in a drought is hard to hold onto, but obedience overcomes the odds.

I saw a powerful example of doing what you know is right even when it does not go your way during the 2018 NCAA Tournament. For the first time in the history of the NCAA Tournament, a No. 1 seed was beaten by a No. 16 seed when UMBC knocked off Virginia in an opening-round game in Charlotte, North Carolina, on the night of March 16. The Retrievers didn't just win the game. They dominated the overall

No. 1 seed by 20 points. It was a shocking result. As the final horn sounded, history had been made, and Virginia basketball was on the wrong side of the story.

As cameras and microphones captured the pure elation and celebration of the UMBC players and coaches, Virginia left the floor in stunned silence. The drought had hit. A painful, difficult, hard-to-digest time had unexpectedly grabbed them by the throat, and the entire country watched it happen.

The game had been nationally televised on TNT, and as you would expect, TNT put in the request to speak with Virginia head coach Tony Bennett shortly after he had reached the locker room with his team. At first Coach Bennett declined the request, as it was not a requirement for the losing coach to speak with the sideline reporter immediately following the game. But as Coach told me a few weeks after that loss, "I changed my mind about 30 seconds after initially saying no because I knew it was the right thing to do."

Like many others listening that night, I was so impacted by his comments to that reporter just a few short minutes after having lost that game. "We got our butts whipped. That was not even close," Bennett said. "A lot of people don't understand that when you step into the arena and you are in the arena, consequences can be historic losses, great wins, and you have to deal with it. That's the job. But we got thoroughly outplayed, did not play well…I don't know what to say, but that was a thorough butt whipping."

No coach wants to be put in that spot, especially after landing on the losing side of history. It would have been the easier path to dodge that one-on-one interview and only do the required NCAA postgame press conference with all media in attendance. But Tony is not about easy. Coach responded to that voice that was calling him to do the right thing, when the right thing had to be very difficult to do.

I have seen it time and time again. The Lord honors and eventually shows favor to those who keep their discipline and make right choices, especially while enduring a drought. I believe that was the case with Coach Bennett and his Virginia team.

I was fortunate to be around that Virginia team on several occasions the season following that devastating loss. I covered them for a week in a tournament in the Bahamas and twice during the ACC regular season. I saw a team that not only survived the drought, but also thrived on the back end. But it did not just happen by chance. That team embraced the loss to UMBC as a time to learn, grow, strengthen, and fight. The disappointment, shock, and anguish that filled their locker room after the loss to UMBC was used in a mighty way.

I spoke with Coach on a couple of occasions about handling that NCAA Tournament loss. The common theme in those conversations with him and his players was "owning what happened." They controlled what they could control and responded with a maturity and humbleness that is hard to find in life. I sensed a thankful spirit for what they had gone through when I spoke with guys like Ty Jerome and Kyle Guy, two key leaders for the Cavaliers. It was a team that was not paralyzed by fear when the next storm hit but instead moved forward with grit and determination.

Virginia was led through adversity by Coach Bennett, whose faith and trust in God was on full display for the next 12 months after losing to UMBC. Getting stuck on why was not an option. Trusting in the sovereignty of God's plan was the choice.

The 2019 NCAA Tournament was a turnaround of all turnarounds for the Virginia Cavaliers. Just over a year after being knocked out as a No. 1 seed in the 2018 NCAA Tournament, Virginia responded by claiming the national title in a win against Texas Tech on Monday, April 8, in Minneapolis, Minnesota. A story of redemption and perseverance had been written. Adversity had fueled a championship. From the opening-round game in the 2019 NCAA Tournament to the final buzzer in Minneapolis, Virginia was tested. Following the 80–75 overtime win in the regional finals against Purdue, which advanced Virginia to the Final Four, Coach Bennett told a national TV audience, "No one knows what this team has been through. I do, and it's good."

Droughts, difficulty, despair, and defeat can be good. I watched it play out for Coach Bennett and Virginia and I have seen it with others as well. But only if the response is proper, do blessings follow the fight. For an entire year, Virginia had responded to adversity and disappointment with grace, humility, grit, and fight. There is no way that response came naturally to anyone associated with Virginia basketball. It was a response that was chosen, and that choice paid massive rewards. "If you learn to use it the right way—adversity—it will buy you a ticket to a place you could not have gone any other way," Bennett said as he and his players lifted the trophy.

I realize losing a basketball game is minor in the big picture of life and what people are facing. But the lesson is there. Search for it, identify it, file it away in your mind, and let it fill your heart with hope. At some point in life, we all will be given a cup to drink from that we want no part of. Your cup will look different than mine. How we handle that cup is what God will be watching.

REMAIN THANKFUL

You have to do it. Nothing pleases God more than remaining grateful during the storm. Being thankful when uncomfortable is a great quality to possess. But this is also where those outside voices have to really help you. I have needed someone to jerk me back into reality more than once when I have found myself in a time of pain and unhappiness. It is so important to get your eyes up and on those areas that are good in your life. Chances are there are a few things you take for granted in your life right now while someone else is crying out to God to provide for them. Read the story of Job in the Bible to understand what I am saying. Though he wasn't perfect at it, he was pretty darn good at praising God and remaining thankful through the loss, pain, and suffering that few will ever experience. I'm not saying to be thankful for the drought; I'm saying be thankful in the drought.

DO NOT FEAR

Fear is potentially a very powerful and destructive word during hard times. Fear can paralyze you and lead to many wrong paths. The actual number of how many times the phrases "fear not," "do not fear," or "do not be afraid" appear in the Bible is debatable and varies based on different translations, but it's a constant theme in God's written word. It is so easy to let fear get a grip on you when day after day it's just not turning around for you. Fear is a very real emotion. Fear gets its grip on our hearts when we forget that God's power and authority are always with us. Your thoughts and your heart can go places driven by fear that you have no need to go. When you are up against the battle of your life—no matter what it is—you have to fight with all you've got to not let your mind settle on that worst-case scenario that may or may not happen. The answer I have for beating fear is prayer that pleads out to God, asking Him to help you hold onto the fact that He will give you whatever you need to face what He has allowed to be put on your plate. You can fear something or you can pray about something, but you cannot do both. Fear is perhaps the enemy's favorite weapon. You have to reject it, or he will pile it on. Do not fear. Do not be afraid. Face it, fight it, pray about it, but do not give into fear and allow it to steer you during those most difficult stretches in life. When you are in a drought, refuse to live in fear. Simply trust that God is looking you straight in the eyes and telling you, "We will not cave into this." Know that God has not forgotten you, and He will come through for you.

DON'T GET STUCK ON WHY?

To be very transparent with you, this one gets a lot of us. It has gotten me for long stretches. I do think it is okay to be completely honest with God and to cry out to Him for answers. But if silence is all you get, you have to move on. Hardships are part of life. Being without problems is not reality. We all face defining moments in our lives, and some of those defining moments will come during the hardest of days. What do you do during the most difficult times of your life? If all you do is ask why, you are running the risk of getting stuck in a really bad place. I have learned this about droughts. If your drought is the result of a poor decision, ask for forgiveness, toughen up, and fight your way out of it. But if your drought is not a result of a wrong decision, you must get to the point where your response is driven by the knowledge that *God allowed this for a specific reason, and I know He loves me, and ultimately this will be good for me.* Maybe there are other ways to view it, but I don't think so. If we always knew why we were suffering, our faith would have no room to grow.

You have to be okay with seasons of brokenness and difficulty in life. It does not make it easier or less painful, but somehow you will get through it. I'm not sure you can ever get past the hurt, the darkness, the trial if you are stuck on why this happened to me. I have experienced a few stretches of dryness in my life, confusing, difficult times that tried to shake my foundation and question God's love for me. It may not be to the extent of the drought you have endured or are currently going through, but I have seen some intensely difficult and dark days. I just know from experience that progress cannot be achieved if you're consumed by how and why did this occur. A drought will drive you back to the basics. We are to love the Lord with all of our heart for who He is—not for what He does or doesn't provide for us. And if He chooses to never reveal to you why something was allowed onto your path and your life absorbed a blow that reached the depths of your soul, we are still called to love the Lord for who He is.

If you have never heard the song titled "Even If" by MercyMe, look it up and listen to the words. That song speaks directly to trusting God, holding on to God, and having hope in Him even when life does not go our way. Here is the first verse:

"They say sometimes you win some,
Sometimes you lose some,
And right now, right now I'm losing bad.
I've stood on this stage night after night,
Reminding the broken it will be all right,
But right now, oh right now I just can't.
It's easy to sing,
When there's nothing to bring me down.
But what will I say,
When I'm held to the flame,
Like I am right now,
I know You're able and I know You can,
Save through the fire with Your mighty hand,
But even if You don't,
My hope is You alone.
They say it only takes a little faith,
To move a mountain.
Well good thing,
A little faith is all I have right now.
But God when you choose to leave mountains unmovable,
Give me the strength to be able to sing.
It is well with my soul."

BE TRANSPARENT WITH GOD WHILE HOLDING HIS HAND

I have had several conversations with God while going through a disappointment, experiencing a deep loss, or a heartbreak. It wasn't really a conversation because it was all one-sided. It was voicing my frustration, my anger, my lack of understanding, my bitterness, my hatred toward some circumstance in my life. Right or wrong, I have been honest with God and told Him I was mad. I didn't know why He was allowing something in my life and questioned whether or not He even cared. It was exactly how I was feeling at the time, so I saw no harm in telling Him. It was just me and God hashing it out. He listened, and I vented.

As long as those words are respectful and still carry an element of proper fear of God and who He is, I think it is not only okay, but also normal. God knows what pain feels like. He hurts with us. I want to challenge you to be very real with God when times are hard. But I will also caution you to remember He is God, and we are not.

He does not owe us an explanation for why something happened in our life. He does not operate that way. I do not know why horrible things happen to people every day who love God with all of their hearts and live lives that honors who He is, but I have learned something very important in my heart. I know God can do anything He chooses to do. He can stop the pain, He can prevent the hurt, He can move the mountain that is standing directly in front of you. But even if He doesn't do any of those things, you can never let go of His hand. Hold on tight as you pour out your heart to Him. Keep a firm grip while confessing how confused and hurt you are and a strong hold while voicing the doubt that has filled your heart. But you can never, ever let go of His hand.

Remember Austin's line about propelling forward, staying strong, doing the right things, and putting others first? That sums up how he battled through his darkest days. It reminds us: when those storms of life blow in and try to break our souls, we have a job to do.

Several months after meeting Austin at the Final Four in Minneapolis, we were discussing one morning how to thrive in the drought—not just simply survive. He pointed me to the Sermon on the Mount found in the book of Matthew. It's arguably the most important teaching by Jesus in His ministry. Matthew 7:24-27 reads: "Therefore, everyone who hears these words of mine and puts them into practice is like a wise man who built his house on the rock. The rain came down, the streams rose, and the winds blew and beat against that house; yet it did not fall, because its foundation was on the rock. But everyone who hears these words of mine and does not put them into practice, is like a foolish man, who built his house on sand. The rain came down, the streams rose, and the winds blew and beat against that house, and it fell with a great crash."

Toward the end of our conversation that morning, Austin said: "We have to do our part. We are taught in the book of Matthew that reading, hearing, even preaching the words of that sermon are not enough. We have to live it."

I have relearned a valuable lesson from knowing Austin this past year. We must do our part and allow God to do what we cannot, especially in the middle of a drought. If you do, I know the day will come for you like it has for Austin, for me, and for countless others that I know. There will be a day where you will be able to look back on those darkest of times, and if nothing else, you are able to express from your heart that you know God is real and always with you. You'll thank him for those days and hours when He was all you had and all you needed. May that never change.

I realize there are many of you reading this right now who are dealing with some very difficult things in your life. Maybe your test is not quite at drought stage yet, or perhaps you are in a place where you aren't sure you can take one more dry breath. Whatever the case may be, understand that sometimes a drought is God's invitation to come sit at His feet and simply hold His hand. Look at your film. Do you have a grip on His hand? Like in golfing terms, is that grip strong, weak, or neutral? If you have a grip, hold it tighter. If you have lost His hand, pursue it. And once you have hold, never, ever let go. Hold on like your life depends on it because ultimately it does. Isaiah 43:2 reads: "When you pass through the waters, I will be with you; and when you pass through the rivers, they will not sweep over you. When you walk through the fire, you will not be burned; the flames will not set you ablaze."

Chapter 6

MAN, THIS PLACE IS ROCKIN'

The quieter you become, the more you can hear.

—Ram Dass

O VER THE COURSE of my 20-plus years with ESPN, I have announced more than a thousand college basketball games at arenas, domes, and gymnasiums all across the country. I am not certain which venue is the loudest I have ever been to on game night, but Allen Fieldhouse on the campus of the University of Kansas; Cameron Indoor Stadium on the campus of Duke University; Rupp Arena, the home of the Kentucky Wildcats; and Assembly Hall on the campus of Indiana University have all rattled my senses at some point or another. The noise level in those buildings can be insane at times.

I have heard the roar inside Tiger Stadium in Baton Rouge, Louisiana, as the opposing team tried to communicate during a one-point game late in the fourth quarter while 102,000 fans shook the foundation of the stadium. There is a reason that Tiger Stadium is commonly referred to as Death Valley. Surveys over the years have all been in agreement. The College Football Association, *The Sporting News*, Gannett News Service, ESPN, and the NCAA have all ranked Tiger Stadium No. 1 in the country at some point as the loudest venue in all of college football.

If you plan on running a successful play in that environment as a visiting team on a Saturday night in the fall, you had better be prepared for chaos and be disciplined in your execution. If a coach takes communication for granted and no plan is in place to overcome the noise, you have no shot at success. And I mean, no shot.

Frank Howard Field at Clemson Memorial Stadium has also wreaked havoc on my ears and opposing teams as well. Also commonly referred to as Death Valley, the original 20,500-seat stadium was constructed in 1941 at the cost of $125,000 or $6.25 per seat. The Clemson Tigers now run onto that field in front of more than 80,000 fans, who impact a game as much as any fanbase in the country. Clemson football has become the gold standard in college football the last few seasons. Their fanbase and raucous environment for home games is hard to match as well.

Beaver Stadium in University Park, Pennsylvania, on the campus of Penn State University can hang with any of them. I remember working the sidelines there one night for ESPN as a sideline reporter for a Penn State home football game. I also remember the producer in the truck telling me to "eat the microphone when you talk on air tonight or you won't be heard." I try hard to maintain great discipline with my diet. I strive to be a team player for my employer and take pride in following instructions. Eating a microphone pushes both areas to the limit. But having worked two games inside Beaver Stadium in front of 106,000 Nittany Lions fans, I know exactly what that producer was telling me with his instructions. If I allowed any room between my mouth and that ESPN hand-held microphone I was using during the game, it would have been a severe struggle to hear anything I was saying. The noise was ridiculous for four straight hours. What an experience!

When I reflect back on other arenas and stadiums that had a similar deafening noise level while I was in attendance, Memorial Gymnasium on the campus of Vanderbilt University has on several occasions been at a fever pitch. That may come as a surprise to many of you—but not to anyone who has been inside that old building on a night where the game is intense and the stakes are high.

Memorial Gym, as it is commonly referred to, is perhaps the most unique playing facility in all of major college basketball. Dedicated in 1952 as a memorial to the Vanderbilt men and women who served in World War II, the arena was built as a combination gymnasium and concert hall. Sixty-seven-plus years later, the unique style of Memorial Gym continues to make the Vanderbilt Commodores' home court a dreaded stop for any opponent. I have personally witnessed many nights of "Memorial Magic" when a capacity crowd envelops the court, which is elevated in stage-like fashion, and deafening acoustics have all had a major impact on the outcome of a game.

One of those games took place back on February 26, 2008. I can vividly remember the ringing sound in my ears as I was walking out of Memorial Gym that night after broadcasting a game between the University of Tennessee and Vanderbilt University. The game was televised in primetime as a part of ESPN's Super Tuesday coverage and, boy, did it deliver.

The Tennessee Volunteers came into the game ranked No. 1 in the nation after knocking off previously No. 1-ranked Memphis just three days earlier on the road. Any Vanderbilt vs. Tennessee basketball game is always a heated in-state rivalry, but this one had extra juice due to the fact that the Volunteers entered the game ranked No. 1 in the nation for the first time in school history.

"Memorial Magic" was deafening for two straight hours that night. Just trying to communicate with the person seated right beside you was a huge challenge. That cliché of "I can't even hear myself think" was truly in play there. My broadcast partner that night on ESPN was Brad Nessler, and during the first TV timeout in that game, he took off his headset, leaned into my ear, and hollered, "Man, this place is rockin'."

And, man, was he right.

Two hours later Memorial Magic had taken down another opponent as Vanderbilt pulled off the upset, beating the No. 1 team in the nation 72–69. It was an instant classic game out of the Southeastern Conference. I am not sure I have broadcast another game since then where the home team's crowd never let off the gas from the opening tip to the final buzzer like the Memorial Gym crowd did that night. It obviously left an impression.

Even on normal game nights, it is extremely difficult for opposing teams to win in Memorial Gym. The fact that the gym floor is roughly three feet higher than where fans are sitting in the first row has a lot to do with it. To make matters even tougher, team benches are located along the baseline under each basket. I do not believe there is another gym in all of major college basketball with this unique design, and as a result, communication between the coaches and players on the court is extremely difficult—and at times nearly impossible.

The ability for a coach to communicate with his or her team is a serious challenge throughout the entire game when playing at Vanderbilt. I am always intrigued by how opposing coaches try to get the attention of their players and communicate with their team under extreme pressure and difficult surroundings. Yelling, stomping, urgent hand waving, and making hand signals are all common scenarios met with inconsistent results.

The head coach for the Vanderbilt men's basketball team from 1999 to 2016 was Kevin Stallings. Over those 17 years as the Commodores coach, he mastered the challenge of communicating with his guys in this type of environment during the course of a game. I watched on many nights, and no matter how deafening Memorial Magic became, he excelled at getting *his* team to hear *his* voice above all the other distractions inside that building.

With two fingers in his mouth and one distinctive sounding whistle, Coach Stallings would immediately get the undivided attention of his guys—no matter where they were on the floor or how raucous and distracting the moment was. His players knew his whistle. It was unique to their ears. Every player embraced the importance of his sharp-sounding blast of passion. It took priority over all the other noise that was fighting to get their attention in that arena. And of equal importance, his players were obedient to his call.

In any sport the call from the coach is crucial. It must be heard at precisely the right time. It must be acted upon with supreme urgency. But first and foremost, it must be heard and distinguished above all other noise. A trained ear is important in sports. The ability to distinguish the right voice from the "almost" right voice is critical. Ears that hear with discernment are of great value to any coach or athlete.

There are lessons to be learned from this example from Coach Stallings and his team that should translate over to our day-to-day life and in particular our pursuit of knowing God. Do you recognize God's voice when He calls? Are you obedient to what He speaks to you? Does God's voice often times get drowned out by all the other noise in your life? Do you listen for God's voice with a discerning ear, a trained ear, like an athlete listening intently to a coach?

That word discernment is key. Discernment is knowing right from almost right. Understand what I just said about hearing

God's voice. That almost right voice has an uncanny way of getting our attention—or at least distracting us from the true voice of God. Satan is the master of deceit, especially in the area of who and what we are listening to. He is consumed with devising schemes to kill, steal, and destroy you and me. Let that sink in for a moment. You and I have the full attention of the enemy. His energy, focus, and schemes are constantly directed toward taking us down. He does everything within his power to get us distracted from truth and God's goodness for our life.

We are bombarded daily with noise and temptations, calling for our attention, and begging us to respond and react in different ways. Often times the noise we hear sounds promising, fulfilling, and innocuous. Noise presents itself in a way that can make it very difficult to not act or respond to its calling. This is where discernment must come into play. You and I must determine the right voice from the wrong voice, and we must know the right voice from the almost right voice. "Almost right" can get you off course just as quickly as wrong. Pray for discernment to know the difference.

We all have multiple signals, numerous voices, and unlimited sounds that are calling for our attention in any 24-hour period. Every waking moment we are surrounded by relentless appeals pulling on us to go in different directions. Consider how many voices every day are calling for your attention. If you and I do not have the discernment necessary to distinguish our shepherd's voice from all of the other noise in the room, where might we be led?

Imagine we are watching that February 26, 2008, game inside Memorial Gym between Tennessee and Vanderbilt.

As we watch the game, we quickly realize that one of the Vanderbilt players seems to be listening to both his coach and the Tennessee coach as the game unfolds. Every other timeout this particular player goes to a different huddle, alternating back and forth between Tennessee's bench and Vanderbilt's bench. Soon it becomes oddly evident that he is being coached and instructed by both his coach and the opposing coach. The opposing coach is clever and deceptive, getting his words in at every opportunity: "Listen to me; my way is better, more enjoyable, and I'll give you more freedom as a player."

How crazy would that be to watch? What player in his right mind would do that? What player would not only listen to the opposing coach, but also eventually believe what he is saying and then begin acting on it? After spending months, if not years, with his coach and teammates, what player would get so confused, so distracted, so selfish, that the voice of the opposing coach would actually attract him? Sure, it sounds like a dumb analogy. That would never happen.

But as unrealistic as that scenario may seem, it unfortunately happens daily, if not hourly, to many who are not locked in to truth and the promises of God. We are deceived by a wrong voice with wrong motives, yielding disastrous results, which can ultimately end up following a call that is based on lies and deception. That's why we must be alert.

Anytime a song rises to No. 1 on any Billboard chart, it is a huge deal. If that song remains at No. 1 for more than a week, it is certainly destined to become a smash hit, joining elite company. But when a song stays at No. 1 for an entire year on any Billboard chart, you are witnessing history being made. That is exactly what singer Lauren Daigle was able to do after releasing her hit song, "You Say" in mid-July of 2018. That song remained steady at No. 1 on Billboard's Hot Christian Songs chart for over a year and rose as high as No. 29 on the Hot 100 list, an extremely high position for a Christian cut on a list of all genres.

"You Say" is a powerful song and sung by a beautiful voice. But I believe the lasting power of that song speaks to a common concern for so many today. The lies we are told by society do not match up with what God says about us. The beginning lyrics are spot on about hearing God's voice:

"I keep fighting voices in my mind that say I'm not enough.
Every single lie that tells me I will never measure up.
Am I more than just the sum of every high and every low?
Remind me once again just who I am because I need to know.
Ooh oh

You say I am loved when I can't feel a thing.
You say I am strong when I think I am weak.
And you say I am held when I am falling short.
And when I don't belong, oh You say I am Yours.
And I believe,
Oh I believe,
What You say of me.
I believe.

The only thing that matters now is everything You think of me
In You I find my worth, in You I find my identity.
Ooh oh.

You say I am loved when I can't feel a thing.
You say I am strong when I think I am weak.
And you say I am held when I am falling short.
And when I don't belong, oh You say I am Yours.
And I believe,
Oh, I believe,
What You say of me.
Oh, I believe.

Taking all I have and now I'm laying it at Your feet.
You have every failure, God, You have every victory.
Ooh oh.
You say I am loved when I can't feel a thing."

I have literally sat alone in my office or in my truck and wept as I have listened to that song. Those lyrics speak straight to the heart of who God is and how much He loves us. It's also a reminder that the enemy is after you and me. The voice of shame, pleasure, lust, and selfishness can be constant. The voice of pride, success, bitterness, resentment, and fear can overwhelm you. I know how loud those voices can be. Trust me. I hear them every single day of my life just like you do.

Those callings inside our heads are determined, ruthless, and adamant, but those lies are straight from the enemy. Satan exists on this Earth to kill, steal, and destroy all or any part of your life that he is able to get a grip on. Again, he watches and studies your film even more than you do. He is against you. He wants to beat you. He searches for an opening to attack. His notes from watching your film are detailed and designed specifically for you. The harm we put ourselves into by listening to the wrong coach in the wrong huddle is potentially devastating.

I have found in my own life that those voices that are harmful, untrue, and pulling me away from God can also be the most persistent at times. Relentless is hard to beat, and remember: the enemy is consumed with his work. If you and I are going to ignore the steady voice of things like lust, greed, pride, insignificance, and fear, we must have awareness, discernment, and a plan. The only way I have ever won any of these battles is through intentional prayer, asking for God's help, humbling myself to know I will fail on my own strength, and responding to the lies I am being told by speaking words of truth about God's promises for my life.

Once your heart is attracted to the wrong voice, it can be very difficult to hear anything else. I have had stretches in my life where every day for a two or three-week stretch I've had to verbalize a specific scripture to drown out the voice from the enemy. Relentless is hard to beat. And those voices that are fighting for your attention—but are not God's best for your life—are indeed relentless. They may not always be the loudest, but they are persistent, and you must understand the danger those voices pose to you as a person. Just as you need awareness, discernment, determination, and a plan to overcome the wrong voice, those same qualities are necessary if you are going to have success in hearing the right voice.

If you want to hear God's voice in your life, you have to spend time alone with Him on a regular, reoccurring basis. Think about it like this: when I sit courtside to announce a college basketball game on ESPN, I have a headset on that is filtering what I hear during the course of the game. The noise level inside college arenas can be deafening at times, making a headset invaluable to all announcers.

About one hour before every broadcast, I will put my headset on and go through an audio test with the audio technician working the game. We are checking to make sure that I can hear several things all at the same time and that the audio levels for each component are correct. It's absolutely necessary that I am able to hear my own voice, the voice of my play-by-play partner, our sideline reporter, the producer, director, and associate producer working in the control room or production truck.

I need to hear the microphones that are strategically placed around the court and arena that pick up natural sound like the officials' whistle, sneakers squeaking, coaches giving instructions, the band performing, the scoreboard buzzer, and shot clocks. The right amount of crowd noise must also be in the mix to help me match the intensity in the building as I break down the game as an analyst. The sheer number of voices and sounds that are coming through our headsets during a live broadcast can be overwhelming if you are not used to the chaos of that much noise. You add all of that intentional sound that comes through my headset and combine it with the natural sound that seeps through due to a rowdy environment, and the challenge to keep it all properly balanced can be difficult.

One voice, however, coming through that headset is prioritized over all of the other noise, and that voice is the voice of the producer. That is the voice that is giving me direction, telling me what replay is coming next, what graphic will run after the next play, when we are going to commercial, and how we are doing as a production team. My ears over the years have been trained to hear the producer over all the other noise. It is critical to my success as a college basketball analyst and critical to the overall success of our shows.

I spend a lot of time with the producer in preparation for any broadcast. I need to know their voice and I need to know the gameplan for our coverage as the show begins. The producer's voice needs to be unique to my ears above all the other sounds and voices in that headset. It is imperative that I hear the producer's call and respond to that call with speed and accuracy. This analogy transfers seamlessly to our day-to-day life. We need intentional ears for an intentional God. That is such a simple concept, but it's one that many struggle to grasp.

So as you begin breaking down your film, what are you looking for in this area of your life? Start with this thought in mind: how much time do you spend intentionally listening for God's voice, reading His written word, and allowing His truth to seep inside your soul? If you don't listen to His voice, how in the world do you recognize it? How can you expect to zero in on His gentle nudge or whisper when the volume of noise in your life is turned up to max? How can you respond to His voice, be led, or changed by it if other voices own your ear?

I challenge you right now to closely evaluate your film in this crucial area. Is it 0 percent of your day, 1 percent of your total time, or maybe 5 percent of your God-given 24 hours in a day that you sit alone with Him? Just 1 percent of your time is only 14 minutes and 24 seconds of every 24-hour period. The remaining 99 percent of your day is going to pull you in many directions. Consistently allow God this time for one week and see how He begins speaking to your heart and changing your life. It's hard for anyone to justify saying you don't have

1 percent of your time (or less than 15 minutes) each day to spend with God. No one is that busy or that important.

During those 14 minutes and 24 seconds you spend with God over time, you will realize He speaks to us in different ways. More times than not, it's God displaying His presence through a gentle whisper, a tug on your soul, a feeling that you just sense over time is the Holy Spirit stirring in your heart. Other times it will be through forced circumstances you have no control over or a conversation with others that can be gentle yet obvious at the same time. You leave the situation or conversation knowing that God intervened and spoke clearly about your direction and where He is leading you.

I also have learned that there will be times that you get alone with God, and you hear nothing but silence. Maybe the scripture you study just doesn't click, and the quiet time is simply just…quiet. Do not doubt, become discouraged, or abandon the journey. Consistent time with God is the key. He loves to spend time with us and He will not remain silent too long. God rewards those who come after Him. You might be thinking: *Jimmy, how do you know that to be true? How do you know what God does and doesn't do?*

It's not something I came up with, read on social media, or heard in a podcast. It is a written promise from God. In James 4:8 it says: "Come near to God, and He will come near to you."

That is an amazing promise from God, a promise that is set in motion by our own action of coming closer to Him. As you study your film in this area, what do you see? Are you doing anything on a regular basis that is drawing you closer to Him? Are you intentional in any way, shape, or form about keeping His voice recognizable and familiar to you? Are you desperate for His voice, His presence, His gentle nudge like perhaps you once were? Are you stuck, retreating backward, or pursuing God? It's one of those three options.

God speaks to us in different ways. Sometimes God whispers, and sometimes God roars. We are given a story in the Bible about a man named Elijah who waited on the whisper. It's the story of a man who had a closeness to God and a single-mindedness about how he lived. In reading the story of Elijah, we see a man who was told by God to go stand on a mountain and listen for the voice of the Lord. Elijah was obedient and went to the mountain. I love the simplicity of that statement.

As Elijah stood on that mountain and waited on God, a powerful wind came and tore the mountain apart. After the windstorm had passed, a violent earthquake shattered the rocks of the mountain he was standing on. When the earthquake was over, a raging fire consumed the mountain. I don't know about you, but if God ever tells me to go stand on a mountain and wait for His voice, and when I arrive, a violent wind tears the mountain apart, an earthquake shatters the rocks, and a fire consumes all that is left, I would be convinced that God had just sent me a message.

But that wasn't the case with Elijah. He had unconventional discernment. He knew what God's voice truly sounded like, so he waited. After the wind, earthquake, and fire had passed, Elijah, who had a trained ear and a sensitive heart, heard a soft, gentle whisper, and that is when God began to speak.

So what do we take from this story? Elijah is no different than you and he's no different than I. Although God did miraculous things through the life of Elijah, the most important part of this story is the very personal relationship and closeness that developed between God and Elijah. You and I can have that same bond with the same God that Elijah did. We, too, can stand in the storms and not be shaken. You and I can recognize the gentle whisper and feel the subtle nudge from God. But just as Elijah did, it will require saying yes to the miracle of knowing God.

To hear from God only in those colossal, intense, blaring moments in our lives just might mean we miss His voice a majority of the time. I sense that God speaks to us these days in a gentle whisper more than any other way. He can often times be heard softly whispering in the quietness of a humble heart during that 1, 2, 5, or 10 percent of your day that you spend alone with Him. If you are going to hear someone whisper or speak in a hushed, soft tone, you need to be extremely close like Elijah was to God. The more background noise there is, the closer you must be. To hear His whisper above all the other noise, you have to be close. I'm talking intensely, intimately close.

God will call us in many ways. He may whisper, but He may also roar with so much volume that you cannot deny He is wanting your full attention. Take Jonah in the Bible for instance. God spoke clearly to Jonah about what He wanted Jonah to do. Jonah heard God, but Jonah did not obey God. He ran from God instead of choosing obedience. Huge mistake. Next thing Jonah knew, he found himself inside the belly of a whale for three days, and the whale took Jonah to where God had instructed him to go in the first place.

Read that story of Jonah again. Let the lesson touch your soul and be imprinted in your thoughts. You might get a temporary pass, and God may display great patience with you when

He is gently leading you in a certain direction. But if God roars and clearly speaks to you like He clearly spoke to Jonah and you purposely choose to ignore it, you just might get swallowed by a metaphorical whale. I do not know what your whale will look like. I do know God is God, and He will accomplish what He wants to accomplish.

Flip back in your Bible to the Old Testament and the story of Samson. It's not good to be remembered for what one might have been, but that sums up the life of Samson. From a young age, Samson had a calling to accomplish great things for God. He began his life with tremendous potential and uncommon physical strength that God had given him. Samson could have empowered his nation and returned their hearts to worship God. He could have wiped out those who stood in opposition of God, but Samson got worn down by a wrong voice. He lacked a consistent closeness to God that would have raised him up above the noise in his life. Samson was taken down by the continuous prodding day after day after day by a woman named Delilah. He put up a decent fight and resisted on his own strength for a period of time, but eventually he caved in, chose his own path, and suffered the consequences for it. Delilah was relentless, which is hard to beat. Over time Samson was worn down and did not listen to God. The trade-off was allowing the wrong voice to multiply in volume and destroy his life. Following the wrong voice was a sad excuse for disobedience.

As you watch, listen to, and dissect this part of your game film, where are you in hearing God's voice? Are you close enough to hear the call whether it's in the form of a whisper or a roar? Is your heart obedient to respond? Do you have discernment in recognizing what is and what is not from God? How quickly do you obey the roar, or is there delay and a lack of response when you know that God has spoken clearly to your heart? Partial obedience is not obedience. Listening with your heart is more important than listening with your ears. Jonah's ear heard God speak loud and clear. His heart did not. Samson knew exactly what God had instructed him to do. He was called to be a Nazirite for life, a person set apart for God's service and a man who would thrive. But Samson had a will to choose and he chose the steady voice of deceit and lies.

That prolonged voice of influence is powerful—for both the good and the bad. Throughout this book I mention the impact those we frequently allow in our ear have on our thoughts, our desires, and our destiny. That controlled group of four or five steady voices that you allow in your ear is critical for keeping you accountable in what you have determined are the dealmakers and deal breakers in your life. But as important as those voices are, they cannot have more impact or carry more weight than God's voice and His Holy Spirit guiding you from one hour to the next.

I know that I personally have direct influence on several men in my life. They look to me for guidance and accountability from time to time. I know God uses me to guide them and speak what I believe to be His truth into their lives. But He is God, and I am not. I may believe with all of my heart and have strong conviction about a particular concern or matter someone comes to me with. But I may miss. God, however, does not miss. His voice has to be the ultimate one that guides you and guides me. Even those, who are closest to you and align themselves with everything you know to be true and reflective of God's word, can unintentionally steer you wrong from time to time.

This whole conversation about hearing God's voice is a constant battle. The arena we live in is loud like a Vanderbilt Memorial Gym kind of loud. The enemy is 100 percent dialed in on how to distract us, what noise to throw at us, and how to effectively keep you and me bouncing back and forth between one huddle and then the other. I know it's hard. I'm in that same arena you are. I understand it. I am fighting through it every day like the rest of us. But we cannot just accept the noise and accept the results. We have to battle.

Your time alone with God is going to determine how you do on this one. You will not recognize His voice above all the other racket in your life if you do not spend consistent time with Him. It simply will not happen. Is His voice above all the others? That's what you are looking for on your film right now.

The challenge is just 1 percent of the time. It is the most important 14 minutes and 24 seconds of your day. Maybe, just maybe, if you look close enough at your film, you will see an opening, a 14-minute and 24-second window of time that should belong to you and God and His written word. Recognizing and responding to God's voice above all the other noise in our life is a severe challenge. To not recognize and respond to God's voice above all the other noise in our life is a severe mistake.

Chapter 7

TOUGHNESS

Opportunity is missed by people because it is dressed in overalls and looks like work.

—THOMAS EDISON

OUGHNESS. THAT SINGLE word is written on whiteboards in locker rooms and above the doors in practice facilities on college campuses all across the country more than any other word I see right now in college athletics. Every coach I know and respect, regardless of the sport, values toughness in his or her team. With coaches from all different levels and sport, I have had numerous conversations about toughness, what it looks like, how you acquire it, and the impact it has on winning. There have been numerous books, articles, and podcasts devoted specifically to that two-syllable word. It's interesting to me that perhaps the most commonly used word in coaching today by high school, college, and professional coaches is actually hard to pinpoint and difficult to define.

I know a tough player or team when I see one. But ask 100 different coaches at any level to define toughness and you will most likely get 100 different versions of the answer. From my perspective as a college basketball analyst, toughness centers around how you prepare, how you play the game, and how you handle adversity. Specifically, tough teams in college basketball are physical teams made up of guys who like contact, hate to lose, accept coaching, compete their guts out, play together, and have a will to win that's hard to kill. Teams that don't let one mistake become two and hold each other accountable in the areas that determine winning are tough teams in my eyes. There are many coaches I have come to know and watch over the years who build their entire philosophy around that one single word—toughness.

One of those coaches is Chris Beard, the head men's basketball coach at Texas Tech University. I first crossed paths with Beard in 1994 while working a college basketball game for

ESPN at the University of Texas on a Saturday afternoon in February. Tom Penders was the head coach of the Longhorns at the time and was kind enough to assign one of his student assistant coaches to drive me to the airport immediately after the game was completed. The game went longer than the standard two-hour time frame, and I had less than 45 minutes to make my flight as I rushed out of the Erwin Event Center to meet my driver, who had been assigned by Coach Penders.

As I sprinted out of the back entrance of the arena, a young man stood waiting on me in the loading dock area. "Hop in, Coach Dykes," Chris said to me. "I'll get you there. I've already got your luggage in the backseat. Let's roll."

And roll we did. He drove me to that Austin airport through heavy traffic 25 years ago with the same passion, urgency, and pace he coaches the game of basketball with today. With time to spare, Chris delivered on his promise. I didn't forget the drive and I darn sure didn't forget the driver. A then-21-year-old Chris made a positive impression on me back then, and it's no surprise to me how high he has risen in the coaching ranks.

I was honored when Coach Beard asked me to come to Lubbock, Texas, in the fall of 2018 to spend the day with him, his staff, and his players. I know how protective coaches are and should be with outside messages and guest speakers being brought in to speak to their team. The fact that I played for and coached with a tough-as-nails coach like Eddie Sutton most likely gave Coach Beard confidence that my message would align with the core beliefs that he has in his program.

I spoke to the Texas Tech basketball family that day for about 40 minutes. Every player, coach, and staff member was in attendance. I shared many of the same principles we are covering in this book with them inside an empty on-campus arena. By the way they listened, I could tell I was speaking to a mentally tough team. I sensed an eagerness for discipline and a hunger for toughness from the entire group. When you speak to teams as much as I do, you can tell quickly what a team is made of by how they shake your hand when introducing themselves, how they maintain eye contact with you as you speak, and how they ask questions at the end of your talk.

I had no idea how Texas Tech basketball was going to fare in the 2018–19 season, but I did know they were a mentally and physically tough group who were driven every day by the 4:1 motto instilled in them by Coach Beard. As I shook Coach Beard's hand and thanked him for having me as a guest, he handed me a black wristband with a white Texas Tech logo and the word "consistency" and that 4:1 ratio number on the sides. "Four parts mental to one part physical is how we approach everything in our Red Raiders program," he said to me. "It's something I learned from my mentor Bob Knight years ago as an assistant under him. The mental is to the physical as four is to one. It means being more mentally tough than physically tough. It's who we are."

I returned to Lubbock a few months later on January 26, 2019 to call the Red Raiders' game on ESPN against the University of Arkansas as part of the SEC/Big 12 Challenge. As anticipated, nothing had changed over the past three months since my last visit to Lubbock. The mental toughness and priority of that 4:1 ratio was on full display as I sat and watched Texas Tech prepare to take on Arkansas during a one-hour practice on the morning of the game.

Every second of the 60-minute gameday practice had purpose, accountability, and intentional stress for every player. Questions were asked about specific coverages and assignments, and answers were expected to be precise and accurate. Energy and attention to detail were demanded and delivered. The expectation for Jarrett Culver, a soon-to-be first-team All-American and lottery pick in the 2019 NBA Draft, was the exact same expectation for the walk-on who would not see any playing time during the game. The team was alert, dialed in, and prepared for a fight.

Honestly, that gameday one-hour practice looked very similar to the majority of the ones I see these days at the major college level. When it's four hours before the game, the pressure and urgency is obvious. I did, however, observe one unique quality in that practice that was different than the countless other gameday practices I have watched over the years.

As I entered the arena that morning, student managers were hustling to set up speakers and a sound system that would rival any nightclub in New York City. As players arrived on the court, the music being played over that sound system on the sidelines was so loud, I kid you not, that you had to literally scream to be heard by someone standing right next to you. The song choices were diverse. The song volume was not. It was full throttle and rocking inside United Supermarkets Arena. Everything from classic rock, hip-hop, R&B, and current and classic country music blared for the entire 60 minutes. The song choices were phenomenal, and the decibel level was deafening.

Sitting between my play-by-play partner, Tom Hart, and our game producer, Scott Matthews, during that practice, I shouted at one point, saying how hard it was to concentrate on what was taking place on the floor. And I knew as soon as I said it, part of what Coach was accomplishing with his team. The music was not only giving life and energy to a team, but it was also forcing them to communicate and concentrate at a level so intense that the game noise that would fill that same arena in just under four hours would simply seem like background noise. He had intentionally placed his team under stress during their preparation. The energy and focus created by that music was unique, and their ability to block out a distraction and perform a task was impressive.

Texas Tech won the game that afternoon 67–64. I did not know at the time how far Texas Tech would advance in the upcoming NCAA Tournament. I just knew it was a hardnosed bunch of guys who were molded from a culture of toughness and honest love from their head coach. Those types of teams are hard to beat, and just over two months later, Beard's team advanced all the way to the national title game in Minneapolis before falling 85–77 in overtime to Virginia.

That 4:1 Texas Tech bracelet that Chris had given me back in the fall of 2018 is still on my desk in my home office. As I began writing this chapter on toughness, I knew a conversation with Chris would give me more insight. I shot him a text on the morning of August 5, asking if he had 10 minutes to talk. He responded later that day, telling me he would call that night. He was busy during the day because he was in Tuscaloosa, Alabama, for a couple days of studying and observing the University of Alabama football program.

The great ones at any level in life are always learning, constantly studying, and consistently searching for ways to get better. Just a few months removed from a national championship game appearance, Coach was right back at it. I could hear in his voice, as we connected by phone that night, how excited and grateful he was for the opportunity to study Nick Saban's Alabama football program. Regardless of who you are, it's not easy to get that type of access. I just think it's really cool how coaches learn from each other these days and how those lessons of culture, winning, and accountability transfer from sport to sport.

I asked Coach several questions during our conversation. Most of them centered around mental toughness and in particular the value he sees in blaring music being played during his practices. "First of all, music gives you juice," Beard said. "We are all about culture, respect, and routine, but we also value fun on our journey. That music has become part of who we are. It does not matter where we are, who the opponent is, or what is at stake in the game. We are going to be us. That music or crowd noise we will also play, it creates a distraction, a distraction that we have to overcome as individuals and as a whole. It creates an atmosphere that forces us to communicate with an intensity that will simulate what we will feel in a game. I believe routine and preparation brings confidence, and that music is part of both. Again, we are gonna be us. The distractions we face have no impact on that."

There is a lot to unravel here. I like the use of the word juice and the value we should all place on having energy and purpose in what we do. Texas Tech has a reputation of a program with grit and fight. But there is an emphasis and awareness within the program of the need for enjoyment in your task. The consistency factor with their music is underappreciated if you don't pause to reflect on it. Home games, away games, neutral floor games, or NCAA Tournament games, Texas Tech stays with a routine, and part of that routine is an intentional distraction while preparing.

When you know who you are as an individual or team, no outside influence changes that. I laughed as Coach told me on their run to the Final Four in Minneapolis that the NCAA did not allow them to use their speakers and loud music on the sidelines during open practices throughout the NCAA Tournament. But routine and preparation breeds confidence in the eyes of Beard. Routines are routines. They are not negotiable or forgotten. So in order to stay true to who they are, Coach had one of his student managers walk around throughout those NCAA Tournament practices with a speaker in his backpack, blasting away the playlist of the day. Often times, society, or in this case the NCAA, will say no to who you are and what you stand for. But culture, belief, and conviction that result from knowing who you are can and should overrule. You find a way to proceed and you ignore the distraction.

Coach and his Texas Tech men's basketball team are just one of many programs out there right now that have a two-handed grip on physical and mental toughness. The process and routine of how Texas Tech goes about it is unique. The transferable message to our own pursuit of change should be clear. The toughest individuals and the grittiest teams have a covenant signed between their heart and their actions. We know who we are, and that will not change.

I hold the highest regard for teams and individuals I come across from time to time that understand and embrace toughness. They have proven to me over and over again how difficult it is to discourage, intimidate, or defeat them. As a former head coach, I would rather play against a team that was more talented than mine but wasn't tough—as opposed to a lesser talented team that was tougher than my own. I would much prefer to coach an average talented player, who was extremely tough, than an above-average talented player, who was soft. I know I am not alone in the value I place on toughness in individual players. You win with tough people. You win in games, you win in building a team, you win in forming a small business, you win in leading a major company, you win as a family, or any other scenario that involves people. When those who are involved have the kind of toughness I am talking about, success will follow.

I mentioned earlier that defining that word toughness can be difficult to do. Outside of the sports world, toughness or lack thereof has a major impact on our lives and those we influence. Some of the toughest people I know have never played one minute of any sport in their entire lives. But they are just as tough or tougher than any athlete or coach I have ever known. I believe toughness can be defined as: *you do what's right when it's hard to do what's right.*

I desire to be one of those people, though I am not always at that level. I want to surround myself with tough people and have their influence on me as opposed to someone who wavers from situation to situation in whether or not they make wise choices. One of the great tests of life is whether or not we continue to do the right thing when it gets extremely hard to do the right thing. Life is going to send difficult trials straight down our path at some point. I'm talking late in the game when you're exhausted, fatigued, and cannot make it through another play, another hour, another day. And when adversity does get to that point, your toughness will be crucial to how well you survive it.

Let's talk about our marriages. My wife is counting on me just like your wife is counting on you. Her heart is set on me being tough and doing what is right when it is hard to do what is right. I am counting on her in the same way. Together, we are trying our best to raise our teenage daughter in a way that the word toughness will define who she is as she grows older. I pray that her heart will desire to do what is right in life when wrong looks really good.

I want my closest friends, the guys I count on for accountability and advice, to have some grit about how they live their lives. I need men in my life who are walking a different path than the norm these days. I do not need the influence of guys who are looking for moral shortcuts. I know the type of influence I need in my life. None of us are perfect, but I darn sure want guys around me on a daily basis who are consistent, resilient, and intentional about doing the right things in their lives. I am very guarded in who I call close friends, and you should be, too.

When I have opportunities to speak to different groups and organizations, I routinely ask them a simple question: who's your five? I have asked my own teams this question on a regular basis as well. What I am asking is this: who are the five people you allow in your ear the most? Who are the five people you choose to spend the most time with? Who are the five people who are influencing your life in the areas of your words, thoughts, attitudes, and actions? That question may be the most important one I could ask you to answer as you look at your film right now. It is that important. I don't care if you are a teenage girl about to enter the eighth grade or a 50-year-old guy who's rolling at the top of his profession. You need to understand how important this next line is. It is impossible to do the right things in life if those you hang with the most are doing the wrong things. I don't care how successful you are, how old you are, or how strong you think your convictions are. You get the wrong voice in your ear at the wrong time, and that distraction will take you down. Out of all the things we are looking for on our film, this one is easy to see and should not be ignored.

At some point in life, things aren't going to go your way. I have lived it and I have learned from it. Especially during those knock-you-to-your-knees times in life, you must be extremely guarded about who's in your group of five. I've had life not go my way. And when those moments occurred, I was very intentional about the five voices I let into my ear at that point in my life. I wanted my toughest friends around me. I needed guys who had strong convictions who I trusted would have no problem telling me what I needed to hear as opposed to what I wanted to hear. I had zero tolerance in those unsettling times in life for anything other than those voices that aligned with the culture and identity of who I wanted to be—regardless of the adversity or circumstance going on in my life. I needed truth spoken to me with conviction and I made certain that is exactly what I heard.

The kind of toughness we are in search of has nothing to do with how physically strong you are, what your pain tolerance is, or the colorful language you choose to use. Instead, it's measured by this: at what point do you opt out, and doing what is right is no longer what you do?

This toughness quality is not common. It is not normal. I believe it is only obtained by intentional actions, unwavering convictions, and an unconventional discipline that separates common from uncommon. Life toughness is earned not given. It is desired by many but owned by few.

I consider myself fortunate to call Buzz Williams a coaching friend of mine. I first met Buzz back in the year 2000 when he was a young assistant coach at Colorado State University. He went on to be the head coach at New Orleans, Marquette, and Virginia Tech prior to being named the head coach at Texas A&M in the spring of 2019. I believe he is one heck of a coach and is one of the great motivators of young men in college athletics right now. Eight NCAA Tournaments in his first 12 years as a head coach backs that up.

I am fortunate to occasionally receive text messages that he shares with everyone in his program. During his final year at Virginia Tech, I awoke one morning to this text message that he had shared earlier that same day with his entire team:

Most of the problems
in the world are the exact
same problems in basketball.
People want to work
in a "normal" way, but
expect/want "unnormal"
results. They want something
they haven't earned.

You guys all understand
this as you read it—

and so would everyone else
in the world.
The problem is they
are not disciplined enough—
not tough enough
to change their daily
itinerary to "unnormal," so that
they earn "unnormal" results.
If there was a pill to skip
the work, and still get the results,
They would sell them.
They have not invented those pills
My heart for you will be the
exact same for you if you
are "normal" or "unnormal"
BUT, my responsibility to you
for your life is to help you understand
that ball and life are really the same.
What you put in is exactly what you
will get out of it.
Don't say one thing and live
Something different. Your words
And your life must match up if your
Goal is "unnormal" results.

I love this text. I think it's cool how he uses "unnormal" instead of "abnormal." Buzz gets it. People naturally want to work in a "normal" way toward something but expect/want "unnormal" results.

Some of the toughest people I know have never been involved in sports in their lives, but they consistently display to me an uncommon resiliency and conviction in pursuing a life with more intention than most. I have great respect and admiration for men and women that I personally know who refuse to have any interaction with their phones, TVs, iPads, laptops, or any form of social media until they have started their day spending time alone with God. That type of front-loading your day is not normal or common.

An authentic walk with God is available to all. The power from His written word still brings change to people's lives. But it comes with a cost, and unfortunately most people want something they have not deserved. If you are not experiencing that closeness to God that you wish you had, why is that? If you say you want a more authentic walk with God, your words must match your actions. What does your film show you? Is there any consistency in your pursuit of God? I know that question can sting, and getting stung can hurt. Growth comes through pruning. Perhaps it's been a while since God's written word has brought change to your life. If there was a pill to skip the work and still get the results, they would sell them. They have not invented those pills. There is simply no substitute for time alone with God. Are you willing to do what others will not?

Unfortunately, God's written word does not scream for our attention the first thing each morning like a cell phone, laptop, and social media does. It's hard to ignore those voices that call to us the split second we wake up. But tough people overcome hard. Tough people are not swayed by the opinion of how everyone else does something. I would put that type of toughness to start the day with God up against any other form of toughness. Having mental toughness based on humility and the conviction to give God the proper place in our lives is unique and powerful. I hope to someday have that type of real strength consistently in my life.

Another Old Testament story depicts toughness in the face of adversity. It's a story of three men who did what was right when doing what was right seemed so costly. In Daniel Chapter 3, the greatest of all the Babylonian kings, Nebuchadnezzar, has constructed an image of gold that is 90' high and 9' wide and set it up on the plains of Dura in the province of Babylon. Nebuchadnezzar had built this statue to unite the nation of Babylon and solidify his power by centralizing worship in his country and ultimately assuring his reign would last forever over his people. By doing so, he rejected God and neither feared or obeyed his commands.

Nebuchadnezzar then proclaimed that every governor, adviser, judge, and appointed official must bow down and worship the golden statue he had made. All but three men did so, and that's where another story of life toughness begins to take place. Shadrach, Meshach, and Abednego were those three men. Those three men, who had been appointed by Nebuchadnezzar to oversee the affairs of the province of Babylon, would not yield, simply refusing to serve the gods of Nebuchadnezzar or worship his image of gold.

We are told that Nebuchadnezzar grew furious with Shadrach, Meshach, and Abednego, giving them the ultimatum to worship his gods and the statue he created or be thrown immediately into a blazing furnace, resulting in the punishment of death. And just like that, a major distraction to who they were and what they believed jumped onto the path of Shadrach, Meshach, and Abednego. This was no minor distraction like a determined fly at a picnic. This was a loud, blaring music, benchmark, pinnacle-level distraction with the ultimate consequence. This was their response, according to Daniel 3:16-18: "O Nebuchadnezzar, we do not need to defend ourselves before you in this matter. If we are thrown into the blazing furnace, the God we serve is able to save us from it, and he will rescue us from your hand. But even if he does not, we want you to know O king, that we will not serve your gods or worship the image of gold you have set up."

That's toughness of biblical proportions.

Nebuchadnezzar responded by ordering the furnace to be heated up to seven times the normal level and immediately had Shadrach, Meshach, and Abednego thrown into the fiery blaze. We are told the fire was so intense that it killed the soldiers as they threw the three men into the furnace.

But Shadrach, Meshach, and Abednego were untouched and unharmed by the fire. God did just as they claimed. He rescued the three men in a supernatural way. God's deliverance of Shadrach, Meshach, and Abednego from that fire was a great victory of faith for many at that time. It should serve as a constant reminder to us to trust God in every situation, through every distraction, and all kinds of adversity.

Shadrach, Meshach, and Abednego stared right through the face of distraction and did not flinch. They refused to change their identity or shy away from who they were even when the stakes were at an all-time high.

So where are you in all of this as you begin to look at this part of your film? I go back to that text message from Coach Williams. Normal these days is common, but it does not mean it's best. I see normal as blending in. Normal is making an excuse or opting out when the road gets hard, the furnace gets hot, or things don't go your way. Normal means more time scrolling through Instagram or Twitter posts rather than time alone with God. Normal is choosing to say critical, mean-spirited things about other people on social media because our hearts have become numb, and we have been blinded to how God views our likes, retweets, and responses. Normal is allowing how other parents raise their children to impact the decisions you make in how you raise your own. Normal is no respect for word choices these days regardless of who can hear.

I am convinced, however, that life isn't going to let up any time soon. It's going to keep coming at you 100 mph, challenging what you believe, testing who you are, and trying to distract you from God's best for your life. Just as Buzz told his players: the problem today is that some people have drifted into complacency and are simply lacking the discipline and toughness required to make a change. Others may recognize they need a new direction and talk about how they want uncommon results but have not in any way put in the effort to earn those results. The majority of people are doing what is referred to as normal, and that is fine. Just understand that you will continue to get normal results in those areas of your life where you are giving a normal effort. But make certain you understand what normal results really look like, according to today's standards. Is that who you want to be?

As your thoughts transition back to reviewing your film, are you tracking normal? Does your heart desire right when wrong looks really good? Is there enough evidence from your film to be charged as someone who does what's right when it's hard to do what's right? Remember, the film doesn't lie.

Toughness is the most commonly used word I hear today when coaches describe the most important characteristic their players can possess. That quality is vastly underrated in our pursuit of God these days. How tough are you?

Chapter 8

BALANCE

We are often tired and imbalanced—not because
we are doing too much—but because we are
doing too little of what is real and meaningful.

—MARIANNE WILLIAMSON

M Y DAUGHTER, KENNEDY, was 8 years old when I left ESPN for three years to coach the University of Arkansas women's basketball team. She asked me two questions the night before I decided to accept the job offer from the U of A, and her first question was a good one: "Do we still get to go to Maui every year?"

Ever since Kennedy turned 2, one of my assignments at ESPN had been covering the Maui Invitational Basketball Tournament held every November at the Lahaina Civic Center in Lahaina, Hawaii. That was the one trip every year that I always took Tiffany and Kennedy with me. When you are 8 years old and all you have ever known is every November you go to Maui for seven days, you consider it a way of life.

I had to break it to her that there would be no more trips to Maui in November but that we would go to some other cool places as a family based upon where my own team would be playing in the future. That discussion lasted for about 10 minutes as she had trouble wrapping her mind around why my team couldn't just play in Maui every year. That's not easy to explain to an 8-year-old kid who grew up going to Lahaina, Hawaii.

Then she asked: "Will you still drive me to school every morning and watch my gymnastics practice at night?" I really realized that our world was about to change in so many ways. I knew the time demands of the job. I had been an assistant coach on the men's side at Appalachian State University, the University of Kentucky, Arkansas-Little Rock, and Oklahoma State University. But I was not married at the time while coaching at those schools, and it was okay to be consumed by work back then. This was different, at least it was to me. I was now a husband and a dad. As a family we had discussed the changes our family would go through with this new job. At the end of those talks, Kennedy had two concerns: Maui and time with her dad.

I called Tiffany into the room after Kennedy asked the second question. I wanted my answer to have staying power and I wanted to be held accountable. I knew exactly the time demands, pressure, and how totally consumed with a job I was about to become. I also knew I was not going to lose who I was in that process. I remember telling Tiffany and Kennedy something like this: "I want both of you to know I am a husband and a dad first. That's who I am. Being a coach is what I will be doing for work, but it's not who I am. My first responsibility and calling in life is to be a husband and a dad. I'm gonna need both of you to help me to remember that going forward."

As we continued to talk, I gave my word to both of them that I would drive Kennedy to school every single morning that I was in town, no matter how late the night was before. I told her I would still come and pick her up at gymnastics and get there in time to watch the end of her three-and-a-half-hour practice every day after school. And for three years, I made good on that promise and kept it a priority. There were many days the only time Kennedy and I spent together was on the car ride to school or driving home from gymnastics at night. But, man, was that time important.

On most nights I left the office and got to her gym around 6:30 PM. I watched her practice for half an hour or more if I could. We headed home after her workout and talked about our day as we drove. I did all that I could to not answer or make calls after we got to the house. I knew I had about one hour to interact and eat with my family before Kennedy would be in bed and I would be back working from my home office.

I was faithful at staying committed to this schedule. It was important to me. Kennedy was 8 years old when I took that coaching job and 11 when I left it. A lot can happen between a dad and his kids between the ages of 8 and 11, and our kids are going to get the attention they crave and deserve from someone or something. One of the first places they will turn to if we are not present in their life is social media. They will look to find their identity through what others say about them. We live in a judgmental, critical, cynical world, and those things thrive on social media where our children live. They are in desperate need of grace, forgiveness, and non-judgmental truth in their life. Where are they getting those qualities taught if it's not coming from home? Stress and pressure can wear us down and result in a lack of time, purpose, and priority in leading our kids. They want our time and need our attention and they are experts at knowing when we are engaged and when we are not.

Many parents fight this battle daily. Life is happening at 100 mph with no exit ramp to pull over, slow down, and reset our pace. The Bible warns us how idle hands and having too much time is grounds for the enemy to attack you. Well, these days, having no time caused by being consumed with your work or the pursuit of a goal is problematic, too, and I know how difficult of a challenge this one can be.

We all have demands on us from a job, a boss, our own expectations, or financial pressures, and if we are not determined to keep balance in our lives, we will underperform in many areas. This chapter may relate to men more than any other. I see the demands many of you are under for different reasons. I have had similar all-consuming thoughts and used that same exhausting energy we feel is necessary to do the job, gain favor with a boss, hit the numbers, make the sale, or grow a brand. When I hear someone say they cannot turn off the work switch when they walk through the door at home, I know exactly what they mean. The pressure to perform and concern that someone is outworking you can drag any of us to destinations God never intended for us to go. As a result, you and I have to decide who or what ultimately determines how we manage our days and where the cut-off point is with our time. Either we set those standards, or someone or something will set them for us.

If work performance is at the top of the list for things that can quickly get us out of balance and off course, No. 2 is likely the emphasis, pressure, and priority that many parents are sucked into making sure their kid is the very best. A number of families I see today are under extreme stress in their lives due to the time, money, and emotional commitment that is being made toward youth sports or competitions. The pressure that families are feeling to keep up with others, who are pursuing the same dream for their child, is intense. I hear from parents a lot these days about the toll a summer travel baseball team, a showcase camp, a dance competition, or an AAU volleyball team is taking on their life, their work, their family, and their relationships.

Erik Bakich is the head baseball coach at the University of Michigan. He led the Wolverines all the way to the finals of the 2019 College World Series before falling to Vanderbilt University in the national title game. Bakich is a tremendous coach and has built the Michigan baseball program into a national championship contender.

During the middle of Michigan's game against Florida State in the 2019 College World Series, Coach Bakich did an in-game interview with ESPN sideline reporter Kris Budden. That interview went viral that night on social media after Bakich answered a question about his mentality when it comes to recruiting. "Well, we just think our roster should look like the United States of America. And so we target a lot of inner-city kids," he said. "There's a lot of great athletes out there, and I think it's ridiculous the cost of travel ball and some of these showcases. And it just, it negates opportunities for a lot of kids. So for us we want to have a diverse roster and we want to provide as many opportunities for kids all over the country that we can."

How refreshing and authentic is that answer? I salute Bakich for his honesty and vision in building his program. I also believe his point about the cost of travel ball and showcases probably grabbed the attention of many parents across the country that night who are wearing themselves out in pursuit of a goal they probably cannot specifically define.

As Bakich spoke on national TV in the middle of that game, he used the word "ridiculous" in describing his thoughts on travel ball and showcases. This is coming from a major college head coach who had his team in the national championship game of the College World Series in June of 2019. He knows what he sees. He has great conviction about how he is going to lead his program.

I am in no way saying that being fully engaged with your kids' activities is harmful or wrong. No one believes in the importance of supporting our children's goals more than I do. But there is a right time, a right season, a proper perspective that should align with pursuing any goal. I live in the real world just like you do. We travel with our daughter for similar events just like you do. I believe it is so important to be committed with your time, your finances, and your positive support to help your children pursue their goals as long as it's their goals—not yours.

I just want to encourage you to keep a healthy balance about dreams for your kids. Be cautious, think it through, make your stance, and hold your ground. Do not be swayed by what everyone else is doing. Step back and observe this part of your film from different angles. What are you truly pursuing and emphasizing to your kids if your family is off at a little league baseball tournament or competing in a dance competition weekend after weekend while missing months of small groups and worship services?

I read a recent study on common traits of Olympic athletes. One of those common areas centered on the high organizational ability of those who go on to compete in the Olympics. They are abnormal in one key area. *What's important right now remains important right now.* How they structure the hours in their day and week are high priority. Time management is not a roll of the dice or determined by the winds of the day.

Our pursuit of how we live life in the season of life that God has us in should be no different. I understand there are times in our work life that we have no choice but to prepare, prioritize, and perform well. You may have seasons or stretches where you have no other choice but to get in early and stay late. I am not ignoring the pressures, demands, and stress that many of us face every single day. Those pressures are real, those demands are heavy, and that stress can be costly. But either you are going to set the standards for your life, or society, a boss, a competitor, or other parents will set it for you. It's your call and it should not be someone else's.

I have been honored to host The Legends of the Hardwood Breakfast at the Men's Final Four the past few years. The recipient of that award at the 2018 Final Four in San Antonio was Tennessee head coach Rick Barnes. I have personally known Coach Barnes for many years, having covered his teams at Clemson, Texas, and most recently Tennessee. Barnes is a phenomenal coach, something that was highlighted by his winning the Naismith Coach of the Year award in 2019, a run of 14 straight NCAA Tournament appearances at Texas, a Final Four appearance in 2003, a regular-season SEC title in 2018, a No. 1 national ranking for Tennessee during the 2018–19 regular season, and by coaching two National Player of the Year Award winners in T.J. Ford and Kevin Durant. The heartfelt words that he shared that morning to a packed ballroom were authentic, fresh, and convicting.

In front of a hushed crowd that morning, Rick shared openly about how God had captured his heart several years earlier and changed the trajectory of his life. As Coach pointed out, he had been raised in North Carolina in a Christian home and knew right from wrong. The crowd laughed when he said, "When you grow up in North Carolina, there are two people that you know: Billy Graham and Richard Petty."

Early on during that 12-minute speech, the entire room could hear the heartbreak in his voice as Rick began sharing about a time in his life when he came to the realization that he was a broken man, chasing the wrong things and ignoring the right things. "What the world came calling," he said, "that's where I went."

Over time the fame, fortune, and vanity that can come to a high-profile, successful person like Rick had taken root inside his heart. As he told the audience that morning in San Antonio, Texas, who he was in private, it did not always match up with what most people saw in public. The enemy's grip had led him to an island of imbalance and wrong priorities in his life.

You could feel the emotion in Rick's voice as he talked about his family and specifically how a daughter is someone you never want to disappoint. One conversation while he was coaching at Texas changed the course of Coach Barnes' life. "'Dad, we need to talk,'" he said, describing the conversation beginning between him and his daughter several years ago. "'We don't like the way that you treat Mom. We don't like the way you are living your life. We appreciate everything you have worked to give us, but we don't want any of it. We don't care about any of it because the most important thing to us right now is that one day all of us are going to die. And if we all died today, Mom and both of your kids would be in Heaven, and you would be in Hell.' When your daughter tells you something like that, it's pretty tough."

I have had many conversations with Rick over the past couple of years. I've heard him talk about going back to former players to apologize for how he led them and how being out of balance and in pursuit of worldly callings once steered his course. I have also heard him tell anyone who would listen about the changing power of the name of Jesus and how God opened his eyes and filled his heart with truth.

I wonder what our film would say as viewed through the eyes of our children? That question may be one of the most important questions we will ever answer. Let it resonate with you for a few days and ask God to give you perfect vision in how you see this.

It is never too late to make changes, accept responsibility, or allow God to reset your heart like He has done for my friend Coach Barnes. I am thankful for the unashamed and transparent words he shared with us at that packed ballroom during the 2018 Final Four. If you were in attendance like I was that morning, your life was impacted, and the Holy Spirit was working in that room.

So what does God teach us about balance and the harm that can come from being off balance? Look at the book of Peter. I love how the amplified version of this scripture reads: "Be sober [well-balanced and self-disciplined] be alert and cautious at all times. The enemy of yours, the devil, prowls around like a roaring lion [fiercely hungry] seeking someone to devour."

Most of the time we think of self-discipline as having the ability to hold back bad behavior. But it's much more than that. Self-discipline can be defined as the control or choice of behaviors, thoughts, or emotions with the aim of increasing the likelihood of attaining long-term over short-term outcomes. It is the ability to display positive, healthy behavior and not just hold back the negative.

I admire those people I come across that display consistent self-control in their lives. Very similar to self-discipline, self-control is restraint exercised over one's emotions, impulses, or desires. That is the opposite of mass controlled or society controlled. If you are self-controlled, *you* are the one deciding what is important to you. If you are society or culture controlled, *others* are deciding what is most important to you, and you chase after those things instead. An out-of-balance person not in control of his or her own life is a primary target for the enemy to attack. God warns us clearly about it in 1 Peter 5:8.

If something is going to be important to you on the last day of your life, you had better make it important to you today. This is true in so many areas, but I believe it is especially important when it comes to spending time with our family. I am talking about undivided attention with the phone turned off and thoughts engaged. It's a time to put away the laptop.

This whole balance thing is a real issue for many. So how in the world do you address it? It will look a little different for everyone most likely, but one common thread will be intentionally resetting your heart and renewing your mind to regain your balance. This most likely will be a fight, but it's still imperative. You learn to compete for what you want while being stressed. You make the necessary changes to gain leverage in the situation and you have the discipline and conviction to stay in the fight until you restore the balance in your life you have determined you need.

This balance battle is going to be won or lost based on your daily choices in some significant areas. Making these choices day after day after day will change the trajectory of your life over time if you just stay after it. Consistency and patience are the key. If you shortcut the process, you shortcut the results.

On a daily basis, it's not healthy to go the entire work day and not call or stay engaged with your spouse. It doesn't have to be a lengthy call, but there is tremendous value in letting your wife or husband know that you are thinking of them during the work hours. There's authenticity and a connection in spoken words that is hard to accomplish through a text message. I understand there are times that texting may be the only option you have, but just be mindful that a one-on-one conversation is still the most effective way to stay connected.

If you have children at home, you have to have a time of purposeful engagement with them on a daily basis. What that engagement looks like will be different according to their age, but it's not just going to happen. It will require energy, patience, and maybe creativity. We give our best effort to everything outside the home. Our best energy of the day, problem-solving skills, and creative thinking are all used on a job or on people outside of our family. You have to flip that. Your No. 1 responsibility, especially as a dad, is leading your home. Don't give your best to others and have an empty tank for what matters most. Parenting is a contact sport. If you are not sure how you are doing in the area of engaging with your children, start by asking yourself this question: *who are the five closest friends my son or daughter has and what are they into?* If you can answer that accurately, you are doing a lot of good things in the area of engagement. If you struggle to answer that question, take note as you grade your film.

Proper daily balance can never be achieved without proper gratitude. Find one thing a day you are thankful for and tell God how grateful you are for it. *It's amazing how much of being out of balance can be tied directly to having an ungrateful heart and lacking contentment with what God has already blessed you with.* I'm all about drive, effort, and passion but not when those qualities are more prevalent in your life than gratitude and thankfulness. Remain hungry but not at the expense of remaining grateful.

On a daily basis, carefully guard your time with God. Do not jump immediately into the noise to begin your day. From personal experience, I know the damage I do to my own life when I become too busy, too prideful, or too self-reliant to give God the proper place He deserves in my life. When I dismiss my time alone with God, some negative things begin to grow quickly in my life. My overall perspective gets out of alignment, God seems distant to me, his promises for my life are quickly forgotten, and God's voice and His will for my life seem irrelevant.

Pause your film at hour No. 1 of the 24 hours God grants you. What are you front-loading your day with? Ask God to set your heart and your mind on the right things, truthful thoughts, and proper direction. Quietly ask God to magnify those areas in your life that truly matter as your day begins. This simple concept produces massive returns if you can execute it.

Secondly, no matter what the day has brought your way, find time each night to turn it all off. The phone, laptop, TV, or iPad can all disconnect us from others in a subtle and harmful way. You cannot be engaged with your phone and engaged with your family at the same time. Listen intentionally, serve others, ask questions. Just be there—not just with your physical self—but with every fiber of who you are.

I had success following through with that commitment to the scheduling agreement with Kennedy and Tiffany when I was coaching. But I failed many nights on spending time in a real, genuine, and fully engaged way. I can tell you exactly where I was sitting and the recruit I was texting the night Kennedy, who was then 10 years old, said, "Dad, you are always on the phone and never listen to me anymore." And you know what? She was right. There were many hours I was home, but I wasn't home. You know exactly what I mean if you are someone with a job that requires much of you and have allowed that job to consume you.

When parents say, "My son or daughter never talks to me anymore," I wonder if maybe that was something their son or daughter inherited along the way from observing their parents at home. It takes discipline and a heart turned toward God in order to stay engaged with your family. I don't believe you have to be in a 12-week Bible study or weekend seminar to get started on making progress on this one. When you are standing in a hole, quit digging.

I have huge respect for people I see who are able to live their lives in a way that reflects who they are and where their priority lines have been drawn. One of those guys for me is Mark Few, the head basketball coach at Gonzaga in Spokane, Washington. I have gotten to know Coach Few by covering his teams on occasion over the past 20-plus years. He is a phenomenal basketball coach. He's been a part of the Gonzaga coaching staff since 1989 and has served that university as the head coach since 1999. During the span of his 30 years on that campus in Spokane, Gonzaga has risen from mid-major obscurity to one of the true elite level programs we have in all of college basketball. "Fewy," as he is known in the college basketball family, has led the Bulldogs to the NCAA Tournament every single season during his time as head coach. Gonzaga basketball is now known as a major basketball power in spite of playing in a league outside of the Power 5 conferences.

Few is the third fastest coach to win 500 games as a collegiate head coach, trailing only Adolph Rupp and Jerry Tarkanian. He ranks in the top five all time for most wins in his first three seasons as a head coach. Coach Few led Gonzaga to the national championship game in 2017, earning AP and Naismith Coach of the Year honors along the way. I view his teams as consistently skilled on offense, tough, and ultra competitive. I have the utmost respect for Few as a coach. I have even greater respect for how he has chosen to go about it.

In the middle of March Madness during the 2018 NCAA Tournament, I heard him being interviewed on a national radio show when he mentioned how he drives his kids to school every morning in Spokane. I was not surprised by his comment, but I did want to talk more with him about the balance he strives for in his life while having an all-consuming job as head coach for an elite level college basketball program. He and I spoke on the phone about a month or so after the 2018 Final Four. I found his comments powerful, authentic, impactful, and transparent. "It haunts me in a very motivating way to think about whether or not I am doing enough for my family as a husband and dad," he said. "It's that same type of motivation that drives me to not lose a game. It's always there. I am not going to be an absent husband or dad. I carve out time for my family. It doesn't matter to me how everybody else may or may not go about doing things. It's a nonnegotiable with me. I'm going to drive our kids to school every morning that I'm in town. When we can, we try to schedule our own Gonzaga team practices so they don't conflict with the practices or games that our own children are involved with. It's not always possible, especially during the season, but I want to be at those practices and games for my kids and I want the same for my assistants.

"I think a lot of guys operate out of fear, fear that someone is outworking them. I refuse to operate like that or allow anyone in our program to function like that. We work efficiently, we have success, but we have determined how we go about it, and staying engaged with our families is one of the priorities in our program. One of these days when I pass this head coaching position on to someone else, I want that standard of sacrifice, competitiveness, toughness, and ultimately winning conference championships and NCAA Tournament games to continue. That is who we are. But I also want that family component passed along as well. It's just not the 'Gonzaga Way' to do it differently."

I know Few fairly well. He is an ultra-competitive guy who has sustained mammoth success with his Gonzaga program. His is an all-consuming job. It's a job he could easily get lost in and allow what he does for work to define who he is instead of what he does. But he is intentional in his approach and has conviction in his beliefs about what are going to be the most important things in his life. You can compete your guts out at whatever you are involved in, sustain high-level success, and win championships without losing your life. It can be done. And Few is one of many examples I know of who are doing so.

Your family is no different than mine. They crave our time, but they are also keenly aware when we are there physically but absent mentally. There are three key areas to look for on film as you begin your balance check. The most obvious one that many are struggling with is the work, which can consume every moment of your day. And when I am talking consume,

I mean it dominates your thoughts, determines your actions, impacts your words, and influences your attitude. Your job can become who you are, and that should never be the case. Your job is what you do—not who you are. Your identity and your significance cannot be determined by your work. If that is the case, chances are you are off balance in other crucial areas of life. I am all about providing for your family, sacrificing, and being disciplined in what you do but not at the expense of neglecting those God has entrusted you to lead, love, and invest in.

Secondly, a hobby can also have you out of balance by pursuing pleasure over purpose Look at your film. How much time are you giving to a hobby each month? I am a big believer in healthy outlets for all of us. We have to have them to maintain our balance. One of my passions in life is working out whether that's running, lifting weights, or cross training. It's also a non-negotiable with me. I am intentional about that one hour a day I give to it. I build my daily schedule so my hobby is not taking away from time I should be giving to other things. I will say it again: I am a big believer in healthy outlets for all of us, but the key is healthy. I don't care what the activity is. If it's taking too much time away from your family, work responsibilities, or time that could be used for serving others, it's not healthy. Are you out of balance between pleasure and purpose?

The other key area that you need to be looking for may surprise you. Are you out of balance in terms of giving? How much of your film centers around you, and how much of your film focuses on others? I struggle with this area. I do not have a natural giving spirit. My film is loaded with examples of making it all about me, what I want, what I need, and what I want to do. My eyes are on me more times than I care to admit, and if they are on me, they cannot be on others. Society is running rampant with that self-first mentality. It's a lie straight from the enemy that many have bought into.

When my life gets out of balance, it is usually due to the fact that I do not have God in the proper place in my life, and as a result, the desires of my heart, my thoughts, my decisions, and actions are all about me. Replay your game film several times in this area. Are you seeing a spirit of giving to others more than a spirit of giving to self? If you are wired anything like me, this part of your film may need to be constantly reviewed. I don't believe you ever beat selfishness, but you darn sure better limit it in your life.

On your last day on Earth, are you really going to wish you had read one more chart, broken down one more spreadsheet, watched one more ballgame, viewed one more episode on Netflix, or scrolled through social media one final hour? I just don't think that's going to be the case. You better start making important now what's going to be important on that last day.

Your son or daughter is no different than mine. You can never allow the pressures of society, a job, or anything else to determine what proper balance should look like in your life. Right is right if no one else is doing it, and wrong is wrong— even if everyone else is doing it. Be right on this one.

Chapter 9

ARE YOUR NONNEGOTIABLES NEGOTIABLE?

Conviction is worthless unless it is converted into conduct.

—Thomas Carlyle

I F YOU HAVE any chance to play basketball for Roy Williams at the University of North Carolina, you have to run, run some more, and run some more after that. Sprinting the court in both directions is a nonnegotiable for Coach Williams and his program. It does not matter if you are a guard built for speed or a big man built to bruise folks. If you do not sprint the floor, you will not play. Every coach I have ever talked to about playing against a Williams-coached team has told me the same thing. If you have any chance to beat the Tar Heels, you have to deal with their commitment to run the floor. It's in their DNA. It's who they are.

Tyler Hansbrough played for Coach Williams at North Carolina from 2005 to 2009. He left the Chapel Hill campus as one of the most decorated and honored players in the history of North Carolina basketball. He was the first player in the rich history of ACC basketball to be named first-team All-Conference four straight years. He was also named a first-team All-American each of his four years in college. Hansbrough was selected the National Player of the Year in 2008 and went on to become the 13th overall pick in the 2009 NBA Draft. He remains one of my all-time favorite college players I have ever had the opportunity to watch play.

He was as tough of a competitor as I have ever seen at the college level. At 6'9" and 250 pounds, he was relentless in his effort and fight. He simply outworked and outran most other big guys on most nights. If I could handpick 10 college players from the past 10 years to have the opportunity to coach myself, Hansbrough would be in that 10. He played the game the right way, and I have tremendous respect for all that he accomplished in that Tar Heels uniform.

I visited with Coach several years ago as he and I shared a ride together from a summer AAU basketball tournament to the airport. During our drive I asked him what made Hansbrough so special. I will never forget his response. "He doesn't get bored with the basics," Williams said.

I thought that was really cool. A four-time All-American selection and National Player of the Year built his career on consistency. He refused to become bored with the basics of the game. Hansbrough was committed to fundamentals. He relentlessly sprinted the floor, went after rebounds with a vengeance, played physically, took great care of his body, and basically just showed up every day and outfought his opponent. Those qualities were nonnegotiable with Tyler Hansbrough as a player at North Carolina, and he ended up being the National Player of the Year in large part because of them. Was he talented? Yes. Was he fierce in his pursuit of the basics? Absolutely. Did he have standards as a player that he simply would not back away from? I believe he did. Excelling at the boring often brings the breakthrough.

I have seen many talented players over the years in different sports, who never reached their full potential or lived up to the five-star rating they were handed coming out of high school simply because they failed miserably at the basics. Boundaries were never formed, standards were never set, and unwavering principles were never established in how they trained, played, or generally lived life. I have seen that scenario: a total disregard for basic skills played out time and time again. Duties and responsibilities that require zero talent are holding people back from getting anywhere close to reaching their full potential.

The discipline required to do basic fundamental tasks over and over again is of great value. Sadly, that type of discipline is the exception in more cases than the norm. Doing the right thing once does not determine success. It's not doing something correctly one time that brings us to victory. It's doing that one thing right over and over again that determines our gain. That daily and consistent grind separates average from exceptional. Perfection of the basics is a narrow road that few people choose to walk on. Long stretches of nothing spectacular will test one's will and reveal one's heart.

Those who excel at the common are uncommon. The grit and fortitude necessary to simply pursue the essentials of any task is rare. Reward comes, however, to those who consistently conquer what many view as simple, minimal, and irrelevant. I am fascinated at times when I see basic beat elaborate, and simple beat complex. Doing what is right simply because it's right. The payoff can be massive.

The 2019 College World Series championship was won by the Vanderbilt baseball team on June 26 at the TD Ameritrade Park in Omaha, Nebraska. Vanderbilt's 8–2 victory against Michigan secured the second national title for the Commodores, who also won the title back in 2014. Vanderbilt baseball has become a national powerhouse and a model of consistency under the leadership of Tim Corbin since he became head coach back in 2003. With 14 consecutive trips to the NCAA Tournament and two national titles in the past five years, Vanderbilt baseball is firmly established as one of the nation's true elite programs.

Vanderbilt was a model of consistency throughout the entire 2019 season. They won both the SEC regular-season title and

SEC Tournament title, set the SEC record for most wins, tied the SEC record with 13 draft picks in the 2019 Major League Baseball Draft, and lost back-to-back games just two times all season long. Talented? Yes. Consistent? No question. Wired a little differently than most teams? I believe so.

About one hour after the completion of that College World Series game, a photo was posted on social media by Brooks Webb, the director of baseball operations for Vanderbilt. That picture and caption grabbed the attention of many, including myself, over the next few days. A simple picture of starting left fielder Stephen Scott picking up trash in the Vanderbilt dugout just after winning the national title told me a great deal about the Vanderbilt baseball program. The tweet said:

An hour after winning a national title in his last collegiate game...

@Stephen-Scott7 stayed & picked up every piece of trash in our dugout.

No one asked him to, & he didn't see me sneak this picture.

He just did what is right

Leaders Eat Last until the end.

@VandyBoys

That's phenomenal stuff. An hour after dogpiling each other in celebration, receiving the national title trophy on national television, doing postgame interviews with the SEC Network and other media in attendance, and finding family members and friends in the stands with whom to capture the moment, a group of talented guys with an uncommon core picked up trash.

That is an exceptional narrative. It's a vivid example of perfecting the humble parts of the game, a real snapshot of what simple standards look like and how they do not change based upon the high or low of the moment. How easy would it have been to ignore the standard for just one night? But that's not Stephen, and that was not Vanderbilt baseball of 2019.

Three weeks after he won the national title, I spoke with Stephen about that picture. I wanted to hear from a tested winner about being spectacular at unspectacular things. Our conversation was every bit as impactful to me as the picture posted the night of the College World Series title game. The carryover for us all should be clear.

My phone rang about 10:00 AM as I sat in my home office working on this book. The caller ID told me it was Stephen Scott, and for the next 20 minutes, I learned in greater depth the importance of details, culture, and the gains to be had from having selfless standards in life.

Within the first minute of our conversation, Stephen made it very clear that he was just one of many in the dugout that night picking up trash. "I just happened to be the one the camera found," he said.

Over the course of the 71-game season, he said, "Probably 71 different times it was a different player to be the first one to begin picking up the trash in our dugout after games. It's just who we are. It's a standard at Vandy. No one picks up after Vanderbilt baseball except Vanderbilt baseball. It starts at the top with Coach Corbin. We have certain things we believe in, things that effect winning that no one sees but us. From the first day in fall ball, our standards are clear and prioritized. We will not waver."

Picking up trash after every game did not win Vanderbilt a national title. But the carryover from that mind-set certainly played a major role. Day after day after day, the team grinded away at those things most ignore or are too prideful and entitled to do. Have you ever been there? Are those simply-picking-up-trash moments few and far between in your life?

I am a firm believer in establishing nonnegotiable areas as an athlete. I have seen the negative results when someone or some group gets bored with the basics. I have watched teams suffer greatly, lose their hope, and ultimately lose their purpose by ignoring the fundamentals, not protecting their core values, and slipping into mediocrity in everything they do. That drift to ordinary can be subtle and slow, but the results are conclusive. If you compromise in the day-to-day nitty-gritty, you lose.

What a way to go down, huh? Ignoring the routine stuff that requires no talent, expertise, or ability other than grinding away at common essential tasks. And yet it happens. Teams fail, individual careers are cut short, companies go bankrupt, organizations go under, and lives are rattled all because values that should be nonnegotiable became negotiable. Could that happen to you? Could it happen to me? Could something so elementary as becoming bored with basic tasks derail us and drastically change the path of our lives? It's a question we need to answer.

Your identity, your brand as a person, what you stand for, and what you value should jump off your film as you begin to view it. Those nonnegotiable convictions that simply steer you through life should not be hard to find. There should be specific areas where a permanent line has been drawn and is not faded, blurred, moved, or crossed. If you currently have these types of lines sketched into your life, now would be a great time to retrace them with a permanent marker and ensure those lines are distinct for you and everyone else around you. Perhaps the list is not long, but surely you have some things that are important enough to you that they have been sealed away in a safe box and not open to compromise or concession. I hope that is the case for you.

If, however, you have never understood the impact of concrete boundaries in your life or lines that have dulled, washed out, or erased, read this chapter with an open mind and ask God to grant you wisdom in how this could be influencing your course or bringing disorder and turmoil to your path.

Our opportunities for compromise are endless. A life without boundaries is a risk. Barriers, standards, and lines that will not be removed, lowered, or crossed are for our own care. Please understand that *God is for you, not against you.* He wants good things in our lives. He desires for us to prosper. His commandments are not holding us back from anything of lasting value. The boundaries and standards He wants to place in our life are for our good, not our harm.

The apostle John says it very well in 1 John 5:3: "This is love for God…to obey His commands. And His commands are not burdensome."

Those commands are not backbreaking, exhausting, fatiguing, or grueling. His standards are not harsh, heavy, painful, or punishing. His boundaries for our lives are not rigorous, taxing, oppressive, or unfair. God's commands are not a burden. His commands, His boundaries, His lines, and

His standards are beneficial, advantageous, profitable, and generous to those who obey.

Are God's commands a burden to you? Are His standards too harsh or inconvenient? Do you view them as out of touch with reality and the pressures of society? If so, why is that? Enduring standards do not fluctuate, fixed boundaries do not move, and permanent lines do not fade. Your nonnegotiable moral code should be written in stone and tattooed on your heart.

The work I do in the offseason and conversations I have with coaches during their down time can be invaluable to me as a college basketball analyst for ESPN. The pressure on coaches to perform and prepare is scaled back to a degree during those months outside of their game season. A coach's mind is a little clearer, the daily pace is a little slower, and conversations during those months often give me great insight in terms of the coach's focus, his or her takeaway from the previous season, and the overall direction of the program.

It's the time of the year that coaches evaluate *everything* in their respective programs. Analysis of the previous season is given high priority and can be tedious work. After countless hours of staff meetings, player/coach meetings, film study, and statistical breakdowns, most coaches also have identified five or six key plays out of the entire season that had a major impact on their team's overall success or failure. Over a thousand different plays and possessions occur during the course of the season. A select handful are always magnified through the eyes of a coach.

We are talking about five or six key plays that occurred at critical times in a game. The trajectory of an entire season is often determined by how well one play or one late-game situation was executed. Those key plays will haunt a head coach if his or her team misfired, but they will fuel confidence for the entire group if winning plays were executed in high pressure moments. Game-deciding, season-altering plays cannot be magnified enough or overstated in the mind of a coach. It's interesting to me how many times a conversation I have in the offseason with a major college head coach ends up focusing on a handful of plays from the previous season. There has to be a lesson somewhere in this for us.

Fran Fraschilla has been a friend of mine for more than 20 years. The former head coach of Manhattan College, St. John's University, and the University of New Mexico has become one of the most respected basketball analysts at ESPN since being hired back in 2003. He and I connect on a regular basis throughout the year just to talk ball, talk life, and bounce thoughts off of each other about specific players, coaches, and teams.

Fran, in my opinion, is as dialed in to college hoops and the game of basketball globally as anyone I know. I learn something from him seemingly every time we talk. I have heard Fran speak multiple times to the importance of making game pressure decisions during the non-pressure days of the offseason. Those plays and situations that can determine your overall success or failure are so important. They are often times dealt with months in advance to ensure advantage and victory is the result.

For example, is a basketball team going to foul intentionally if it is up three with less than 10 seconds to go in the game, thus forcing the opponent to shoot free throws instead of a potential game-tying three-point shot? If a coaching staff comes to the conclusion in the offseason that fouling when protecting a three-point lead gives their team the best chance to win, then other questions must be answered as well. Where on the court are they wanting to commit the foul? How do they execute the foul properly? What determines who they will foul on the opposing team? How much time on the clock should there be when they foul? These types of decisions should be made far in advance of this actual situation occurring at the end of a game. The pressure is intense, stakes are high, and there are just too many variables to consider when you are making these decisions on the fly during the final 10 seconds of a game.

In football it equates to situations like when should a team go for a two-point conversion after scoring a touchdown or when to take an intentional safety as opposed to risking a punt when protecting a late-game lead. Pro golfers will often predetermine a certain club to hit off of a particular tee box—regardless of the circumstances of the round or what place they are in overall in the tournament. That decision is made before the tournament ever begins, and it's all based upon the conclusion they came to while playing the low pressure practice rounds days or weeks in advance while preparing for that particular part of the course.

Decisions made in the offseason, during practice rounds, and during those low stress parts of the year often times are the difference in success and failure in sports. There is wisdom and foresight in taking this philosophy from sports and transferring it to our own life choices.

I have great admiration for those who make life pressure decisions far in advance of life pressure moments. I'm talking about people who have established some clear standards and have unwavering convictions in certain areas of their lives. They have identified areas that are potential game savers or momentum changers in their lives, predetermined how they will respond when those situations occur, and then consistently executed the plan time and time again. These people do not change their stance based on circumstances, what society screams is right or wrong, how they physically or emotionally feel on a certain day, or any other variable that life may throw at them.

I am thankful to have several men in my life who are like this. I appreciate the consistency they display to me on a regular basis and the impact it has made on how I strive to live. I have a core group of guys in my life that excel at the basics. Their lifestyles may or may not wow you, but they wow me. I am wowed by consistency, and this group of men I am talking about have a tight grip on that word.

I see tremendous wisdom in having nonnegotiable standards, deciding far in advance of that situation actually occurring, knowing what your response will be, and then performing the plan with skill and conviction. When pressure situations, compromising opportunities, or sudden temptations cross your path, you need to be clear, concise, and confident of what action you will take. There can be no hesitation. You quickly pull the right club out of your golf bag, you hit the ball safely in bounds, and you proceed to the next shot.

To live life with no limits, boundaries, or time to make offseason decisions regarding what is allowable in your life is a risk. It's like a non-prepared coach entering a season, hoping he guesses correctly in the biggest moment of the game. *Hope is not a plan.*

Let's put our eyes on some nonnegotiable boundaries that deserve our attention. I've found some of my boundaries to be crucial to where I am trying to go as a man. They include diet, physical fitness, who I will spend time with and where that time will be spent. I understand this is about as fundamental as it gets, but I stay alert to not get bored with the basics, lose the core of who I want to be, and neglect those things I control. Tyler won the National Player of the Year with a similar gameplan. I have also determined it a priority to read something daily to encourage, grow, or challenge my faith.

Now let's dig a little deeper. I have decided to never leave the house in the morning without praying with my wife and daughter. It is a nonnegotiable in my life. I was challenged to pull it off about 10 years ago, but it's now a daily part of our home's routine. It does not change based on how late we are running or what the frustration level may be in our home on some mornings. We pause, hold hands, and pray.

We give our day to God and say thanks for who He is, the blessings in our life, and for the promise of salvation for those who believe in the death and resurrection of Jesus. I ask for His hand of protection and favor to be upon me and my family throughout the day. I ask for His Holy Spirit to lead us and guide all three of us in all that we will do that day.

I believe in the power of prayer and have seen its impact on my life. The act of praying every morning with my family has changed our home as much as anything we have done over the past decade. I have seen it change the homes of others as well. In less than a minute, each morning we give God the place

He deserves to begin our day. It's my responsibility to lead my home. If the leader of a home isn't placing God in the proper spot, who is?

Even if no one else in the entire world prays with their family each morning before leaving the house, though that's hardly the case, I would remain unfazed. I just know it's non-negotiable with me. We are going to start our day and end our day praying together as a family. The circumstances of that day and how stress free or stressful the day may have been have no bearing. We are going to humble ourselves as a family and pray, knowing we will fail miserably without God being the center of who we are.

Let's zero in on things that can drastically define who we are and where our path might be headed. If a standard is not set, it could unsettle your foundation and collapse the walls of your life. You are now looking for those five or six plays throughout the year that have to be scripted out in advance of them occurring in your life. Those plays you anticipate are coming and could derail your season if you are not prepared and execute properly. Those handful of situations will haunt you if you fail or fuel greater success if you conquer.

I do not want to condemn anyone right now. I am addressing this topic as a reminder for myself as much as anything I have written so far. But I do want you to stop your film and see the potential impact of these plays in your life. Not everyone is going to see this chapter the same or agree with every word. What I have determined as nonnegotiable for me may not be for you at this time of your life. That is fine. All head coaches are different in what they emphasize and demand from their team. Not every head coach places the same priority, the same value on the same things when evaluating the overall health of their program. That's where discernment needs to come into play right now. Allow God to open *your* eyes to what He wants *you* to see. Discernment is not knowing right from wrong; discernment is knowing right from almost right.

I understand this book is not full of fluff. You are not reading chapter after chapter by an author who is telling you what you want to hear instead of what you need to hear. The enemy loves fluff. I do see how determined the enemy is. I have seen the results of complacency on men's lives. I want you to win whatever battle you are currently fighting or about to fight next week, next month, or next year. Soft and easy prepares no one for a test. Any coach who loves his team will intentionally stress them in preparation for the opponent.

What boundaries have you established for yourself while traveling out of town for work? Where is the line drawn on those hunting, golfing, fishing trips with your buddies? In-town boundaries and out-of-town boundaries should be identical. What does your film reveal?

I was recently playing in a fund-raising golf tournament, and one of the guys in our foursome began asking me about my work and how I handled life on the road. After giving my response, I was anxious to hear if he traveled much with his job. His answer was spoken with conviction and without hesitation. "I used to travel three to four days a week," he said. "But now that we have three small kids at home, I just don't want to be gone like I used to. I mainly don't travel anymore because the temptations on the road were starting to affect my life. I told my boss that I could not do it anymore, and if it cost me my job, then it cost me my job. Thankfully, he moved me into a new position that requires very little traveling. On those rare occasions I do travel now for work, my wife goes with me."

And then the next thing he said really stuck: "An unknown man in an unknown town is the recipe for problems."

I thought that statement was authentic, truthful, and relatable to many. If you have yet to establish nonnegotiable standards in your life, no place will test you quicker than being away from home. Your guard gets let down, your thoughts run in different directions, and the voice of the enemy gets turned up in volume. That "no one will ever know"voice has a crafty way to turn your heart in a direction you never intended to go.

I want to go back to the conversation I had that day on the golf course. You may think asking for a change in your job or taking your wife on the road with you on those occasions when you do have to travel is extreme and unrealistic. Maybe that's the case but maybe not. I see it as a man who recognized where he was headed and was determined to change the path. I listened to a guy that day who has established nonnegotiable boundaries in his life that simply will no longer be crossed. I was challenged by a man who put his own selfish desires behind him so his family would not suffer from his actions. I saw a guy who made a pressure-packed life decision in advance of that moment occurring. This man now reaps the benefit of that offseason decision.

Maybe you don't travel for work. The enticement of being out of town with time on your hands is not a series of plays you need to deal with. Do you, however, have a boundary regarding who you will go to lunch with while at work? Surely, that's no big deal, or is it? I know a substantial number of men that will not be in a room one-on-one with a female co-worker. Either the door is always open, or another person is called into the meeting. After reading that sentence, some of you are probably thinking, *That's not even feasible.* Perhaps you are correct. But is it possible the enemy has you complacent, numb, and just a few thoughts and steps away from disaster?

Off the top of my head, I can name at least a dozen guys I know of who will not ride in a vehicle by themselves just one-on-one with a member of the opposite sex. You may say that's ridiculous and totally impractical. I say it's a nonnegotiable standard for these men who have made life pressure decisions during a non-pressure time of their lives.

Where is your line when it comes to responding to a text message? In particular, I'm referring to that one message you know in your gut has the potential to take you somewhere you should not be going. I will say it for you since some of you may be thinking it. *Just texting isn't going to take me somewhere I never intended to go. That's ridiculous.* Possibly.

But we have all heard stories that began with the words: "At first we would just text every now and then. It was no big deal." I will tell you what is a big deal. The enemy loves a slow fade to the slaughter. That is a big deal and worthy of allowing it to sink into our souls and change how we operate. The enemy hates you and loves when you show complacency, pride, and ignorance to his schemes.

Setting standards, boundaries, and barriers helps us prosper in many ways, but perhaps none greater than this: nonnegotiable lines will keep you where you need to be—and just as important—keep others from crossing over into an area with you. That statement is so simple, so elementary, but it's oftentimes ignored. Have you ever been there? Are you there right now? Has that line faded or been completely erased? Don't just move on or brush those questions aside. Pause and give specific reflection.

I can almost sense some of you reading right now are wanting to skip to the next chapter or put this book down and be done with it. Please understand the point of addressing these issues is not to shame or guilt anyone. The point of highlighting these types of plays on your film is to at least make you pause and consider: is there a better way for me to go about this situation when it occurs? Focus in on those you interact with on Facebook or Instagram. Are those interactions above board and appropriate? It's a yes or no question.

Ask yourself right now—in the quietness of your heart—*does any of this apply to me?* Film evaluation can be hard to watch and painful to work through. Don't let difficult stop you. Proceed ahead and hold on. What are you watching on your phone or computer? Things just got real.

I know this one is tough. I also know it has its grip on hundreds of thousands of men every day. I watch lives being ruined, marriages breaking apart, kids losing their dads, dads losing their jobs, and the enemy is the only one winning. Perhaps nothing is more important when we are evaluating nonnegotiable boundaries and barriers than what we allow our eyes to see. The options are endless. Our conviction and discipline will be severely tested on these plays in life.

Gus Malzahn was named the head football coach at Auburn University on December 4, 2012. The 2019 season was Malzahn's seventh year overall as the leader of Auburn football. He and I have been friends since the day I hired him as the head football coach at Shiloh Christian High School in Springdale, Arkansas, in 1996. Back in the mid-1990s, I was beginning my career with ESPN and was also serving as the athletic director at Shiloh Christian, a small private school in the heart of Northwest Arkansas. Gus quickly transformed Shiloh Christian football into one of the most dynamic high school offensive teams in the nation. In 1998 his Shiloh Christian team set a national record at the time with 66 passing touchdowns for the season. Shiloh won back-to-back state championships in 1998 and 1999.

Gus has always been known as a developer of quarterbacks throughout his career. As the offensive coordinator and quarterbacks coach at Auburn in 2010, he coached quarterback Cam Newton to the Heisman Trophy and first overall pick in the 2011 NFL Draft. Gus and I were talking one day about football and life when the subject of quarterbacks came up. I remember him telling me, "The great ones, the difference makers are great with their eyes. They have tremendous eye discipline with what they look at before, during, and after each play."

He went on to talk about how important it is before the ball is snapped for a quarterback to see and read protection. A quarterback has to locate where the defensive backs are lined up as an indicator to where the pressure may be coming from when the ball is snapped. On certain plays Gus described how a quarterback must be trained to have his eyes directed down the middle of the field in order to force defensive backs to play honest, thus slowing down their ability to read and react to where the football is being thrown. He ended that part of our talk by saying, "Discipline with your eyes is the foundation of playing the position."

I find that statement to be simple, wise, and transferable to our lives. Not only is eye discipline essential in order to be a great college quarterback, but I also believe that the eye discipline Gus talked about in football is a tremendous challenge in life, especially for men today.

I'm not even going to attempt to tell you what you should and shouldn't be looking at. That's for you to determine as the Holy Spirit leads you. I just know the importance of nonnegotiable standards in life. I understand that discipline with your eyes is a common foundation for effectively playing the position of quarterback at a school like Auburn in the Southeastern Conference. I also believe discipline with your eyes is a cornerstone for the position of husband, dad, and follower of Jesus in today's world.

Nothing has its grip on the hearts of men more these days than where their eyes are going on a consistent basis. May God speak directly to your heart on this with the love and concern that only a father can do. Please pause right now and speak this out loud: God is for me, not against me. Keep repeating that line until it consumes your heart. Change will come in your life. Lay your convictions at His feet and allow Him to work.

I am certain this chapter has been difficult for many. Hard stops most people. Don't be common right now. Thank God for what He has spoken to your heart about. Authentically, tell him you need His help, His truth, and His cleansing in your life. Win those five or six plays that have been derailing your life.

I'm not perfect in my execution of the nonnegotiable areas I have determined for my life. No one is. I still have times where I boldly walk right up to that no trespassing line I personally established and see how far I can go. I will walk on that line and on occasions cross over it. But, thankfully, by the power of God working to change me, when those times do occur, my spirit is uneasy, my peace is taken away, my heart is troubled, and the whisper of His voice gets my attention much quicker than it used to.

I want to emphasize again the importance of grinding away day after day at basic, essential things. I could write an entire book dedicated to grinders, men and women who just refuse to downplay the importance of the essentials in life. They stand out, their path has a uniqueness about it, and the impact of their life is magnified far and above the norm.

One of those grinders I have had the pleasure of knowing is the late Mike Slive. I got to know Slive on a personal level in 2007. For the first time in my career, the majority of my game assignments with ESPN were in the Southeastern Conference that year. Slive served as the commissioner of that league from 2002 until his retirement on July 31, 2015. Under his leadership for 13 years, the SEC rose to unprecedented levels of success and prosperity. He orchestrated benchmark TV deals, which included the launch of the SEC Network. He led the tradition-rich SEC through expansion of its members by adding both Texas A&M and Missouri. The revenue generated under his guidance was astounding. When he took over as the SEC commissioner in 2002, the league was bringing in $96 million dollars as a conference. When he retired 13 years later, the league was raking in well over $300 million annually.

He was a driving force behind the college football playoff system and served on the NCAA men's basketball selection committee. His accomplishments and influence in college athletics could be an entire book all by itself. He was one of the most powerful men in sports but also had the rare gift of connecting with people that few in a position like his ever embrace.

About one year prior to Commissioner Slive's retirement, George Schroeder wrote in *USA TODAY* about the rise of Slive from his days of laying concrete and working as a meat cutter while paying his way through law school to his position as one of the most powerful men in all of college athletics. But tucked away inside that *USA TODAY* story was a glimpse of who Slive was—not what he did. Shortly after waking up around 4:50 AM to start his day each morning, he would take the time to handwrite a note to his wife, Liz, before heading off to work. He would write down his itinerary for the day, talk about how much he had enjoyed the evening with her the night before, what he was looking forward to after work, mention personal things between him and his wife, and then on the bottom sign it: "I cherish you."

I believe those early morning notes from Slive to his wife of 50 years were nonnegotiable for him during most likely the busiest time of his career. It is so true. We make time for what we value.

Commissioner Slive passed away on May 16, 2018 after a three-year battle with prostate cancer. He was a leader. He was tough, creative, kind, and passionate about his job and how he treated people. He lived a life that displayed to me the importance of nonnegotiable standards to live by. Slive had perspective and life balance. He was a grinder in the basics like the simple act of a handwritten note day after day after day.

I want to encourage you to right now spend time alone with God and ask Him to speak to your heart about what your nonnegotiable standards should look like. Welcome the Holy Spirit to renew, reeducate, redirect your thoughts, heart, and decisions in this area of your life. Pray for the strength and determination to execute those decisions day after day after day. Draw a line and don't move it.

You are never so far down a path that you cannot turn around. I love being around people who are walking through life with a limp, a limp that was the result of a hard fall or stumble. Those folks are real. Their stories are impactful, their convictions are authentic, and their destiny has been forever changed. Remember God is for you—not against you.

Chapter 10

GUARD YOUR HEART

As I walked out the door toward the gate that would lead to my freedom, I knew if I didn't leave my bitterness and hatred behind, I'd still be in prison.

—Nelson Mandela

HAVE A BLACK T-shirt hanging in my bedroom closet that I see almost daily. In bold white lettering across the front of that shirt are the words "Guard Your Yard." I have never worn that T-shirt, but it may be the most important shirt I have ever owned.

That T-shirt was given to me as I walked out of Rupp Arena in Lexington, Kentucky, one night after announcing a college basketball game on ESPN between Kentucky and Texas A&M. It was handed to me by a high school coach who lives in the state of Kentucky. He explained to me that he had them made after listening to me one night during a broadcast talk about the importance of "guarding your yard" while playing defense in a basketball game.

I thanked him for the shirt and for taking the time to find me. As we ended our brief talk, I reminded him that nothing is more important in basketball than the ability to guard your yard. I encouraged him to demand it from his players, make it the No. 1 priority for his team defense, and not to compromise in that area as a coach. "It will determine your success," I told him.

What I mean by guard your yard is that if you are the defender guarding a player with the ball, you *cannot* allow the person you are guarding to dribble right past you on a direct path to the basket. This type of straight-line drive by the offensive player is a killer to team defense. No other principle of playing defense is more important than this very basic concept. If you allow straight-line drives to the basket in your man-to-man defense, you are also creating a series of problems with your team defense. It's just that simple. If you cannot contain the ball but instead allow it to be dribbled right past you in that 3' space on either side of you as a one-on-one defender, several things are happening to your overall defense, and none of them are good. You are going to get beat on a consistent basis. That's why you have to guard your yard.

But I have not kept that shirt over the years to remind me of how important it is to properly guard the ball on a basketball court. I understand that concept well. I have, however, kept that T-shirt in front of me as a reminder for something much more important. When I look at that shirt from time to time, it triggers a thought with me to *guard my heart* in every facet of my life.

Nothing in basketball on the defensive end of the court determines success more than guarding your yard. And when we draw the correlation between guarding your yard in a basketball game and guarding your heart in life, the takeaway can be life altering. Everything begins in our heart. Our contentment, peace, fears, word choice, values—along with things we hold animosity toward, worry about, lust after, and resent all originate from the core of who we are. Good qualities and bad, they are both constantly jockeying for position and fighting for space in a very crowded room. If it all begins in our heart, how should we go about protecting something so valuable and significant?

We must first establish that we determine what is allowed into our heart and what is not. I cannot protect your heart for you any more than a teammate on the bench can guard your yard while you are playing defense in a basketball game. That teammate can encourage you, but he cannot do your job for you. That principle holds true in basketball and it holds true in life. You have the responsibility to guard your heart. It's a job that cannot be delegated or passed on to someone else. Proverbs 4:23 says: "Above all else, guard your heart, for it is the wellspring of life."

Those first three words should grab our attention. "Above all else" means it is the top priority and deserving of our full attention. Notice in particular what follows those first three words. It does not say to worry, be anxious, compare yourself to others, guard your friend's heart, impress others on social media. We are clearly encouraged to guard *our* heart, the dwelling place from which everything in life flows.

The desires of your heart directly impact the direction of your life. Your heart has no secret that your behavior won't eventually reveal. If bitterness is growing in your heart, you will respond out of bitterness at some point. Allow lust to simmer in your heart and you will act out of lust in some form or fashion. If fear is consuming your heart, your performance will be driven by anxiety, worry, or unease. And if things like humility, gratitude, and selflessness are thriving in your heart, you will react to life in a humble, gracious, and selfless way. What is allowed to establish residence in the depths of your soul will ultimately be acted on.

I mentioned the word fear as one of the specific traits that can steer us off course. I want to expand on it briefly. I have personally experienced and witnessed the destructive power of being influenced by an anxious heart and a fearful spirit. The enemy loves to see alarm, anxiety, despair, panic, and uneasiness growing in the heart of a person, and he will do all he can to feed you fear in hopes of it spreading wildly out of control in your emotions, your thoughts, your words, and your soul. You can *never* allow lies that originate from the enemy to settle into your heart. Those untruths, deceitful thoughts, and deceptive attacks must be recognized and uprooted immediately, and fear is one of the most powerful lies that the enemy will try to use.

Consider how many times in a day you are offered up a lie that is centered around fear. The enemy is relentless with his pursuit of trying to fill your heart with dismay and worry. The enemy, the accuser, the one intent on destroying your life, will do everything he can to poison your heart. Worry, anxiety, and fear are some of his most effective assaults, and allowing them to grow and flourish in our hearts steals away the peace and truth God has for us. You can worry about it or you can pray about it, but you cannot do both. What does your film show you about that statement?

Grade your film right now. What is seeded, developing, and threatening to spread in your heart at this very moment? If a job or position you have desired for a period of time has not come your way, perhaps God sees something that is lacking in your heart as opposed to what's lacking on your resume. Doubting God and not trusting in His sovereignty and timing in your life is starting to consume you. How did those feelings get in, and when and where was the door cracked?

Have you flirted with a desire instead of fleeing from it? Though that desire hasn't established roots yet, the truth is that it's threatening to make your heart its home. Possibly there's something that's been lingering in your heart for a period of time and is now beginning that new growth stage. Roots are beginning to spread. It has not blossomed into an action yet, but the increase is obvious, and it now consumes a major part of your thoughts and desires.

Examine your heart closely and consider the cost. Pride, fear, selfishness, anger, bitterness, lust, and envy will not be content to just live passively in your heart without creating action. Those damaging qualities have never been content to sit passively in our hearts. They never have and never will. You are not going to be the one exception to this rule, and neither am I.

If something is thriving in your heart that has the potential to destroy you, it will destroy you if not removed. You may be able to delay that hurtful response or harmful action that comes from an infected heart for a brief period of time just off sheer determination and discipline, but if you do not intentionally fend off those invasions that the enemy has designed for the purpose of taking you down, they will take you down.

Our hearts are a battlefield not a playground. They were not built to be a fantasy walk-in closet where we place secret desires, wrong attitudes, and cravings for sin, and expect no harm to be done. Our hearts are a daily arena where a war is being fought between right and wrong. Protecting our hearts is serious business.

If your heart is anything like mine, it allows straight-line drive at times from vices like selfishness, greed, lust, and envy. I will resent it when others get what I wanted and felt I deserved. My significance in who I am will be confusing at times, and I will judge my significance based on the wrong things. I will compare myself to others and I will allow society or social media to influence how I see myself as a man. I will judge others quickly. It's an endless list of things that are poison to me, transgressions that will attack my heart in a split second or slowly take me captive over time and set up shop.

And the only person who can keep that from happening is me. Proverbs 27:19 says: "As in water face reflects face, so a man's heart reflects the man."

Think about it this way: any time poison is involved in our lives, the speed that it is recognized and dealt with is critical. Urgency becomes a priority. No one waits until next week to seek medical care if they just accidentally ingested a known poison into their body. As soon as it occurs, immediate action is taken. Poison is poison, no matter the form it may come in, and our heart is no different than any other part of our body. Protecting our heart and acting quickly when it comes under attack is of vital importance.

Nick Nurse led the Toronto Raptors to the 2019 NBA title in his rookie season as an NBA head coach. One of the first things he did as head coach was establish a "get-it-out" mentality with his players and coaches when it came to dealing with grievances that can attack any team or organization. I have heard Coach Nurse talk about this mentality on more than one occasion. A 30-year journey as a college coach, British Basketball League head coach, two-time NBA D-League Coach of the Year, and assistant coach in the NBA obviously prepared him well for the moment. You don't coach a team to the NBA title unless you are dialed in on all facets of the game, and Nick managed the chaos of an NBA season exceptionally well in his first year as head coach.

From the day he was introduced as the Raptors coach on June 14, 2018, Nurse made the importance of communicating quickly with one another when players or coaches were offended in some form or fashion acutely clear to his players and staff. He wanted everyone in that Raptors organization to be comfortable with what he called "saying hi" to the elephant in the room. The purpose was having the trust and confidence to deal with issues quickly and properly when they did occur instead of ignoring the elephant and allowing issues to linger. I believe there is much to be learned by Coach's approach.

As a reminder to keep this get-it-out mentality prioritized throughout the season, Coach Nurse had a small ceramic elephant in his office that players and coaches could place on his desk at any time to simply indicate they wanted to talk. That's really cool. An organization built around highly motivated people, who are the best in the world at what they do, was able to put egos aside, kick pride and arrogance to the curb, and talk through issues before they become a cancer to its cause. The goal was clear and simple: don't ignore hard issues when they come up, eliminate blaming others or the situation, and be proactive as a team in not allowing harmful feelings to linger. Address the issues and discuss them in a positive manner.

That mentality did not win the NBA title for the Raptors. The versatility and elite talent of Kawhi Leonard, the toughness and tenacity of Kyle Lowry, the length of their defense, and the selfless togetherness of how they played the game were much larger factors. But I am convinced that get-it-out mindset when it came to dealing with potential poisons throughout the course of their season played a role as well.

We would all benefit greatly by placing an elephant in a chamber of our hearts as a daily reminder to quickly confront the wrongs that somehow trespass into our hearts before they have time to dwell, take hold, and cause damage. What does your film reveal here?

I challenge you to look for a few key words and concepts on your film as you search for the true condition of your heart. Mind-set, technique, tenacity, responsibility, and mental toughness are all common phrases I hear repeatedly from folks I have gotten to know personally over the past 20-plus years working for ESPN. It is extremely rare for me to have a conversation with those people and for some or all of those words not to be used. Let's plug these words into the pursuit of a clear heart and soul to help reveal where we are in this pursuit.

What is your mind-set about the importance of guarding your heart? How much does it concern you? Does it concern you at all? Do you have a plan when it comes to protecting what you desire and allow into the depths of your soul? How about tenacity when it comes to protecting your heart? Do you fight to keep your heart pure and controlled by the promises of God or do you simply allow anything and everything to have a straight line to the core of who you are? Technique and tenacity have to both be in the mix if you value the condition of your heart.

Have you accepted responsibility for what is currently controlling your heart, or is there a theme of blaming others for your disappointments, sins, and regrets? I know actions or words by others can be damaging, cruel, and vicious. I am not ignoring how real, how deep, and how difficult hurt can often be. But you and I are still responsible for how we respond to others. A heart that blames is a heart that's stuck, and stuck means progress is nearly impossible.

And finally, what kind of grade would you give yourself for *mental toughness*? Are you gritty enough to fail but come right back the next minute, the next hour, the next day even more determined to silence the lies that try to get a piece of your soul? Pause for a moment to be honest and transparent with yourself. Are you allowing straight-line drives by harmful things directly to your heart? I can help you answer that question by asking another question. Is there any resistance at all from you when it comes to allowing wrong desires, harmful fascinations, or hurtful cravings to seep into the core of who you are? How easy is it for lust, fear, jealousy, anxiety, or a critical nature to settle into your foundation? Are damaging appetites blowing right past you like a poor defender guarding the ball in a basketball game, resulting in others being put in a bad position as well? What you allow into your heart impacts those closest to you. Your inability to place a hedge of protection around your heart puts others around you in harm's way as well.

I was told by a wise elementary teacher that if success is to be achieved in the classroom, you must find multiple ways to teach the same lesson. Similarly, let's look at guarding our hearts from a different perspective. The word culture can be defined as the attitudes and behavior characteristic of a particular group. Culture is revealed in who you are, what you value, and the actions that follow. Culture is a word with tremendous impact. That is a word that deserves your attention and is determined by your heart.

If you and I could sit down and have a 30-minute conversation with any successful person in a position of leadership or influence today, I can just about guarantee that at some point in that conversation the word culture would be used. Visit with a high school coach, who is winning state championships, or a college or professional coach consistently in the hunt for a national title or world championship of any sport. Gather thoughts from the CEO of a thriving company, the principal of a top 10 nationally ranked academic school, or any leader who is impacting thousands of people daily, and they will at some point talk about the culture they are trying to change, build, or maintain. These people know that the collective heart of the group drives the attitude and action of the team, company, school, family, or any organization you can think of.

During that 30-minute conversation, they would also mention the amount of energy spent daily to either change a bad culture they inherited or to keep the culture they desire in place. Culture is a daily battle. You don't just one day achieve great culture and then move on to the next fire to be put out or goal to be met. Expect culture to be hard to obtain, expect the challenge to be frustrating, and expect the process to be met with resistance. But also expect massive returns from a flourishing culture that has been redirected by a changed heart.

Individuals and teams that possess an above-all-else mentality when it comes to culture are thriving in what they do. Above all else, what is the desire of your heart, and what actions are being created off of that desire? Study your film.

What kind of culture are you pursuing as a person? Do you even know? Have you ever thought about it? Does it even matter to you, or are you just existing in life with no plan or understanding of the condition of your heart? Have you considered how detrimental that could be to you and to the culture you are building as a person? If you want to just barely get by in life, then just barely give your attention to what your heart is turned toward and the actions that follow. I see so many people struggling in life because they have allowed harmful thoughts, lies from the enemy, and discouraging words from others to take hold of their hearts and drastically change the course of their lives.

You may be reading this with a heart that was contaminated with poison early on in life due to circumstances that you had no control over. Being part of a broken family or the victim of abuse, neglect, or the loss of a loved one are all capable of leaving unwholesome effects on our hearts and imprints on our lives. These types of situations are real, and if they occurred at a young age, you can inherit damaging deposits that you had no control over but still must one day be dealt with. Similar to a new coach inheriting a team with bad attitudes, values, and beliefs, you didn't cause the issues, but you do need to deal with them and reset your heart and soul, your culture, and your destiny.

As you continue conduct your own self-inventory, consider a few other traits, which can unhinge and unsettle us. Would you describe yourself as having a thankful heart when you spend time with God or an asking heart built around a wish list for what you desire for God to do for you? What does your game film look like here?

Do you see someone with a selfish, prideful, or perhaps arrogant heart? Those types of hearts fuel the energy in teams with bad culture. We should learn from their mistakes. What type of culture do you currently have when it comes to pursuing God in your life? What is the true analysis of your heart in this area? Do you possess a heart that at one time desired to spend time alone with Him, but now it's no longer a priority?

You may have a complacent heart toward God, but He does not have a complacent heart toward you. He loves you. He desires to spend time with you. If complacency toward God has settled into your heart, you've allowed it to happen. I know because I have been there. Other things have found residency in your heart and are now taking up the space that once belonged only to Him.

Prospering, thriving culture *never* just happens. It is developed over time. And whether we are talking about an individual who desires a culture of trusting God with greater depth or a team that wants to develop a culture of toughness, the pursuit of culture requires constant awareness, relentless stalking, and constant protection once it is obtained.

In the book of Genesis in the Old Testament, there's a beautiful story about a young man who protected his heart with uncommon vengeance. If anyone mentioned in the Bible had a right to own a hardened and poisoned heart, it was Joseph, a man who rose in power from slave to ruler of Egypt all due to his ability to guard his heart and a personal culture that pursued and trusted God in all situations.

Joseph was sold into slavery at the age of 17 by his 10 older brothers. He spent 11 years as an Egyptian slave and two years in prison before rising to the position of governor of Egypt at the age of 30. Joseph was kidnapped, rejected, betrayed, forgotten, sexually tempted, falsely accused, enslaved, and imprisoned unfairly. But through it all, Joseph protected his heart. The hardships he experienced never once settled into his heart. Joseph stonewalled bitterness, resentment, anger, and pity with great success. Molded by pain and a heart that was turned toward God, Joseph survived and prospered when many would have failed miserably. Joseph owned a personal culture that withstood the test. A protected heart produced actions that were rewarded. Toward the end of his story, Joseph was able to graciously forgive his brothers and shared his prosperity with them. It's a testament to how God graciously forgives us even after our own unfaithfulness to Him. Two qualities that changed Joseph's life would change ours as well.

Anything that stands in the way between you and the culture you are trying to build has to be dealt with directly. Anything that is standing in the way of you and the heart you desire to have must also be dealt with in this exact same manner. I believe God will speak directly to you on this subject as you continue to break down your film. It may be about one specific area or it may be several. I do know this: God does his greatest work through a heart that is humble.

Before you turn the page on this chapter and dive into the next, I encourage you to spend time alone with God for multiple days in a row. Ask him to search your heart, reveal to you the roots of poison that may have crept in, and claim the powerful name of Jesus to help you remove those poisons.

That is why a T-shirt that I have never worn just might be the most important shirt I own. I need a constant reminder of protecting what my heart desires and building a culture inside of me that is pursuing the right things. When you evaluate those things in your life that ultimately determine your path, your success, your failures, and your destiny, nothing is more important than guarding your heart, where the wellspring of life begins.

Chapter 11

PARTIAL OBEDIENCE IS NOT OBEDIENCE

The ship that will not obey the helm will have to obey the rocks.

—ENGLISH PROVERB

"**Y**OU MISSED THE line." That is perhaps the most commonly used phrase in all of sports by coaches from all walks of life. You would have to search long and hard to find a football, basketball, soccer, volleyball, or tennis coach at the high school, college, or professional level that at some point in their career has not said those exact four words. And more times than not, it is immediately followed by: "Back on the line, do it again."

If it's a sport that requires sprinting, agility, or running stamina, every team in the country must go through a period of training where the primary focus is getting each individual athlete into top physical condition. These workouts are accelerated in intensity just prior to the beginning of the playing season. These types of conditioning workouts will typically involve some form of a running drill that requires an athlete to sprint and change directions going full speed. On a basketball court, these types of conditioning drills are normally referred to as line drills or suicides. On a football field, they are commonly called gassers. Tennis coaches refer to this type of conditioning as side-middle-sides. No matter what you call it or where the drill is taking place, line drills, suicides, side-middle-sides, and gassers will put intentional stress on an athlete both physically and mentally.

These types of drills require all out sprinting, touching a line on the court or field, and changing directions after touching the line. It is inevitable that someone is going to shortcut the drill and fail to touch the line before changing directions. Sometimes an athlete may miss the line by a full step and other times by an inch, but through the eyes of a caring coach, it all looks the same. "You missed the line" will be shouted with passion and conviction every time a line is missed. The drill will be repeated until each individual athlete touches every line throughout the entire sequence. I have seen this type of conditioning workout go on for much longer than the intended time. Twenty minutes of conditioning can escalate quickly to a half hour or 45 minutes. Players get mad at coaches, coaches get frustrated with players, and players blame each other for the lack of execution. All of this happens over the simple fact that one athlete refuses to do what he or she is supposed to do—touch the dadgum line!

Why is something as basic as touching a line during a conditioning drill so important to a coach? Why do coaches harp on athletes who miss a line by just two or three inches? Why does that even matter? How could something that seems so small and takes place weeks or months before an actual game or competition make such an impact on a coach and how they view individual athletes? It's because you cannot win with someone who is looking for a shortcut or the easier path. You cannot trust someone with the big things that affect winning if you cannot trust them in the small areas that affect outcomes. When the pressure is on and the game hangs in the balance, the difference between winning and losing is razor thin. It's very difficult to have success at the level you are capable of having if you are counting on someone who has a track record of *almost* doing it right. That statement was true 50 years ago, and it will be true 50 years from now. *Almost* gets you beat—plain and simple. I have heard the argument from athletes, saying that missing a line by an inch or two is no big deal. Well, they are wrong.

Missing the line gives a coach great insight into how much heart, toughness, discipline, and accountability an athlete truly has. It doesn't matter if we are talking line drills, suicides, and gassers, or we are evaluating the discipline in our lives regarding what God has asked us to do. Partial obedience is not obedience. You either touch the line—or you don't.

As I have written this book, God has dealt with my own heart about multiple things that need my immediate attention. There are key areas where I am missing the mark, refusing to take that last big step or final three inches that are required for full obedience. Maybe God is doing the same for you. As you have read through the previous chapters and graded your film, you have recognized things that are not quite right, imperfections have been brought to light, and for the first time in maybe a long time, you feel a tug on your heart to turn course and change direction in some area of your life. And now a decision has to be made. Are you going to step on the line or come up short by a few inches or feet? What has God spoken to you about in the previous pages of this book? Has your heart been touched in a way that you know it's God's hand trying to lead you in a new direction? Do you almost want to be committed? Do you almost want to forgive? Do you almost want to stay inside those boundaries you know good and well you should stay inside of? Do you almost want to lead your family in their pursuit of knowing an authentic God? Do you almost want to hear God's voice? Do you almost want to survive the drought? This all comes down now to a choice, a choice of obedience or no obedience. Allow God to change your heart or resist God and remain unchanged by His calling.

Obedience is a choice, and it's one we all must face. It is one of the few things in life we can control. If you have seen on your film an area where you are not submissive to what

God has spoken to you about, why is that? Partial obedience is not obedience. You either touch the line or you don't. The sinful nature in all of us will make excuses and try to justify almost touching the line or at least getting closer to the line than you were before. What our sinful nature will not tell you is this: our Heavenly Father loves us more than we can imagine or comprehend, but He gives us a choice in life to love Him in return, and loving in return requires obedience. John 14:15 says: "If you love me, keep my commandments."

A powerful story of complete obedience is told through the life of Joshua in the Old Testament. Continuing with the story I referenced previously, there's a lesson on how God views obedience and the consequences for coming up short. This story begins in Joshua chapter 6 when God instructs Joshua, the leader of the Israelites, on how he is to lead his people in taking down the walls of Jericho and ultimately destroying the entire city. God is very specific about how this is to occur, giving Joshua an unconventional way to conquer an area that was considered invincible and a symbol of power and strength. Joshua is obedient to what the Lord instructs him to do, and as a result, the city of Jericho is taken down just as God had promised. But there is one small problem, and that small problem has a major impact.

God was clear-cut and definitive about what was to be done with the remains of the overtaken Jericho. The silver, gold, bronze, and iron that remained in Jericho were sacred to the Lord and were to be set aside for His treasury—and His treasury only. Everything else was to be destroyed and left behind. When God says everything, he means everything. When God shouts touch the line, He means touch the line.

Joshua, however, had one man in his army who came up short. His name was Achan, and missing the line came with an extremely high cost.

Achan made a choice, and his choice was to disobey what God had ordered. Achan coveted and took expensive robes, gold, and silver during the capture of Jericho. He secretly brought them back to his family's tent and placed the items with his own possessions. So on the day that the walls of Jericho came crashing down, everybody touched the line except one man, and God was not pleased.

Due to Achan's disobedience, we are told that God was angry and removed His hand of favor and protection from Joshua, his people, and his army. As a result, Joshua's army was routed in their next battle, one they should have easily won but instead were defeated because God was not pleased with Achan and the direct defiance of His commands. Soon after losing that battle, God spoke to Joshua, telling him, "I will not be with you anymore unless you destroy whatever among you is devoted to destruction."

God was specific and God was clear. He would not protect Israel's people until the disobedience was removed and the entire army returned to obeying Him without reservation. This was a massive army, an army that had only one disobedient man out of approximately 30,000 men. You could argue the army was obedient overall, only missing the line by a single inch. Yet God was angry and called for the one who disobeyed.

Early that very next morning, Joshua did what he was told to do. He called out to his followers and found Achan to be the one who had been disobedient. Achan's mistake was disobeying God's specific command to destroy everything connected with

Jericho. I think it's interesting that Achan did everything as instructed during the battle of Jericho right up to the end until he saw an opportunity to keep a few possessions for himself. But God is not content with us almost doing what He asks. Thousands of men were obedient on that day when the walls of Jericho came tumbling down and the city of Jericho was destroyed. Achan was the exception. One man, who coveted what he could not have, caused massive destruction to himself and others.

This story of Achan may seem extreme. After a stretch of obedience, one man's disobedience does not seem fair. After all, Achan did everything he was required to do right up to the end. His story is a very strong reminder that partial obedience is not obedience. Not in the eyes of God. Achan simply missed the line, and it cost him everything. So why did God not allow anyone to keep treasures from their conquest in Jericho? He doesn't just ask us to jump through hoops for no purpose.

When God demanded that Joshua and his army destroy everything in Jericho, He did so because the people of Jericho were living a serious life of rebellion against God, and God viewed this rebellion as a threat to Joshua and his people. God's plan was to ensure anything and everything associated with that rebellious spirit was eliminated and did not have a chance to spread and grow throughout Joshua and the Israelites. God is serious when it comes to sin and God is serious when it comes to obedience. Ultimately, God is serious about his love for his children. Many struggle with stories like this about a God who can seem too harsh at first glance with his children. But if you look closely throughout the entire Bible you see a larger picture of a father who loves his children so much that he will do whatever it takes to ensure that they do not wander into dangerous territory—even if that means allowing temporary pain and suffering in order to prevent a more permanent poison from seeping in. God loved his people too much to allow self-destructing behaviors to infiltrate the group, and so the entire city of Jericho was dealt with because of this.

When God speaks to your heart, Achan's heart, Jericho's heart, or my heart, He does so because He loves us and He cares deeply for us. He does not ask more from us than what we are capable of doing. If he is speaking to your heart about a specific area, it's because He knows what is best for you in your life. God doesn't want less for you. He wants more of what truly can make your heart happy and content. Perhaps you are wrestling with a thought like, *I know God has spoken to my heart and I now see a mountain in front of me that I know needs to be dealt with.*

I understand mountains and I understand mountains that won't seem to move. But it may be time to start looking at that mountain from a different perspective. Don't see the mountain as being in your way. Look at that mountain as it is your way to knowing God in a way that you have never known Him in the past. That mountain, that change you know is needed, *is* your way to a deeper, more authentic walk with God. Again, it is going to be a choice. Climb the mountain or avoid it. I will caution you that God seldom moves a mountain for us, especially when that mountain is for our own good. He loves us, but He gives us freedom to make choices in our lives. And when the mountain standing in your way is a call to obedience, nothing pleases Him more than when we choose to start climbing.

So what do we do? Our hearts have been spoken to, God has clearly opened our eyes to concerns and sin that needs our attention, but the task seems massive. Thankfully, we serve a massive God. In our own strength, we will fail. But our Heavenly Father understands, and He is pleased when we come to Him. Don't overthink it. Get quiet before God and tell him you are limited in your own strength. Confess to God your sinful ways. In simple layman's terms, just tell Him you need His help. He will show up. And when He does, suddenly it will be down to just you, God, and a mountain that has to be dealt with.

I do know of some specific occasions when God showed up and moved a mountain in someone's life. It happened in Biblical times and it still happens today. But more times than not, God shows up with an axe, a rope, a pair of spiked shoes, and tells us to start climbing. And now obedience is in the equation. It's you, God, a mountain, and a call to obedience. Will you climb or will you not?

If God decides to change the size of the mountain and lighten your workload as you begin to climb, so be it. But if not, you remain obedient to what you know He is calling you to do and you keep climbing. And you climb, climb, and climb some more. The size of the mountain has no impact. You touch the line and you choose obedience.

We are all dealing with something. Life has a way of throwing confusing, painful, and heartbreaking things our way. Just look around where you are right now: the guy sitting next to you on the plane, the young mom sitting across from you on the other side of the pool, the couple drinking coffee at the next table over. We all have stuff. Everyone has difficulties and uncertainty in their lives. That is not going to change. Our response to life is what God has His eye on. And when our response has only one of two options—obey or disobey—God watches closely. God is not asking for perfection, but He is asking for us to grow in our faith, our trust, and our obedience to His voice.

Some of the most powerful figures in the Bible all had times where obedience and disobedience were both options on the table, and obedience was the choice that was made. Look at the stories of Moses, Noah, and Abraham. All three had mountains to climb, conditioning drills to complete, and lines to be touched. All three took God at His word, made the choice to obey, and trusted Him with the outcome.

Let's look closely at Abraham in particular and what there is to learn from his trial, his mountain, and his obedient response. In the story from Genesis chapter 22, God tested Abraham.

After struggling for years to believe that God would deliver them a child, God delivered on His promise, and a son was born to Abraham and his wife, Sarah. Abraham was 100 years old when their son, Isaac, was born, and Abraham loved his child dearly. When Isaac had grown to be a young boy, God spoke to Abraham one day and told him, "Take your son, Isaac, the one that you love, and go to the region of Moriah and sacrifice him as a burnt offering on one of the mountains I will tell you about."

I admit I do not know why God would ask this from Abraham. There are things in God's written word I wrestle with from time to time, stories and situations that are confusing to me and areas I don't quite understand. What I do understand is this: God is God, and I am not. Some day it will all be clear to me, I am sure. But until that day comes, I can only control what I can control and trust in Him is one of those areas.

Abraham's story continues early the next morning after God had spoken to Abraham about sacrificing his son. Abraham got up, saddled his donkey, took two servants and his son, and headed off to the region of Moriah. There was no hesitation from Abraham. He heard God speak and he obeyed. Had Abraham delayed that journey by a day or two, he may not have gone, and the line may not have been touched. My instincts tell me that had he delayed his obedience, Abraham most likely would have talked himself out of it, rationalized that the request was too difficult, listened to the wrong voices around him, and questioned God to the point that his delayed obedience would have transitioned to disobedience.

As you continue reading the story, you will see that God ultimately did not have Abraham sacrifice Isaac. But what you will see is that God was pleased with Abraham's response, his immediate answer to obedience, and his complete trust in God. Abraham's obedience impacted the history of the world, and through that choice of obedience, God ended up richly blessing Abraham and his descendants. I wonder what blessings we miss as we deliberate and pause after God says to move.

I encourage you to possess an Abraham-like response in any area that God has spoken to you about while reading this book. There are so many things that occur in life that we have zero control over. But we do control our obedience. We either touch the line or we don't. As it says in Hebrews 11:8, "By faith Abraham, when called to go to a place he would later receive as his inheritance, obeyed and went, even though he did not know where he was going."

Over the past 20 years with ESPN, I have traveled across the country to a handful of college campuses each fall to watch college basketball teams practice in preparation for the upcoming year. Watching different teams work out in late September and early October provides me with a jump start on the season in terms of which teams or individual players are going to make an impact on the national landscape of college basketball. I try to absorb as much as I can during these early season workout sessions, making notes on trends and priorities that coaches are emphasizing with their individual teams.

These early fall practices are often the first opportunity for me to see some of the highest rated incoming freshmen in college basketball, players who will have a major impact on their teams' success and most likely enter the NBA draft after just one year of college ball.

Lexington, Kentucky, home of the Kentucky Wildcats has become a consistent destination for me each fall, as John Calipari, the head basketball coach at Kentucky, has consistently signed recruiting classes loaded with high school All-Americans and future NBA players. I have observed future top NBA lottery picks like John Wall, DeMarcus Cousins, Anthony Davis, Michael Kidd-Gilchrist, Nerlens Noel, and De'Aaron Fox all struggle with the pace and intensity of an early-season workout under Coach Calipari. I sat and watched Derrick Rose struggle during his first workout under Coach Calipari at the University of Memphis back in 2007, as he began his journey to becoming the No. 1 overall pick in the 2008 NBA Draft.

Watching a Kentucky practice in late September is often an old-school coaching clinic, as Coach Cal teaches and instructs with a purpose and passion that is designed to speed up the process of becoming a team that is capable of winning Southeastern Conference championships and ultimately a Final Four.

During the first week of October back in 2011, I sat and watched Coach Cal drill his guys at a rapid fire pace throughout a 90-minute, early-morning workout. The energy was high, Cal's voice was intense, and the urgency to get better was obvious. Toward the end of that workout, Coach Calipari blew his whistle, and the floor became silent. "Anthony, what are you doing?" Coach Cal shouted to Anthony Davis, one of three *Parade* All-Americans in his 2011 freshman class. "I have no idea what you are doing," continued Cal, as he walked toward the 6'10" forward, who would go on to become the National Player of the Year, a first-team All-American, and Most Outstanding Player in the NCAA Tournament for a Kentucky team that would win the 2012 National Championship. "I don't know what you've been listening to or what you are watching in our film sessions, but that's not how we do it here."

Coach Cal then took a minute to show his star recruit exactly the footwork he wanted off of a pick-and-roll play designed specifically for Davis. As Cal walked back to the sideline, he blew his whistle again as the gym once again fell silent. "Listen, all of you, but particularly you freshmen," he said. "I am not going to hold you accountable for the things we have not gone over and worked on. We have a ton of stuff that we have not gotten to yet. It's October, it's early, we are throwing a lot at you. I get it. But I am darn sure gonna hold you accountable for those things we have gone over since Day One and things you should know. Every one of you has to take responsibility right now for listening, learning, and doing your job. I am not asking you to do someone else's job. I am asking you to do your job and I am holding you accountable to do what we have taught you to do. Do your job!"

I believe that is where we all are in life. God is holding us accountable for those things we know, and we are responsible for those things we do understand. And as you have watched your film, have you seen those plays where you are missing your assignment? Not every situation or topic we have discussed in this book applies to everyone. God has all of us on different timelines on our journey to know Him. However, if God has clearly spoken to your heart, and your film has revealed areas that need changed, then there's no other way to really put it. You are responsible for your response. Will you do your job or will you not?

As we close out this book, I want to take us back inside that film room that was described back in chapter one. The film has now been watched, teaching points have been made, and instruction has been given. The lights are turned back on in the room at the request of the head coach, as he makes his way to the front of the group. Mature, tough teams with winning cultures and discipline are alert, the body language is engaged, and there is an energy for learning. Individuals are challenged by what the film has revealed—not resentful, hostile, or bitter. The hunger and thirst for improvement has increased, and a thankful spirit for honest teaching and feedback is present. The room remains silent as the coach begins to speak. You can sense that accountability has been demanded, and progress is going to be made.

Immature teams, on the other hand, with a losing culture and fake toughness are distracted in their thoughts, the body language suggests a lack of caring, and the room does not feel connected or engaged with what was just discussed and shown on film. You get the feeling around these types of teams that excuses are the common thread, a rebellious spirit fills the room, and individual acceptance of accountability is extremely low or completely missing. Resentment and hostile feelings grow inside individual players. Improvement and change are talked about by the head coach, but the words he speaks fall on prideful ears, and no change will come about.

Place yourself inside that film room. Which response are you most likely to give as you reflect on what God has spoken into your heart? It's extremely rare to see players or entire teams in a film room that are a little bit of both. There is a clear distinction in that room between those who desire change and those who do not.

We are prone to stray. God is prone to pursue. Perhaps that is what is taking place for you right now. God is pursuing your heart in a new way. He is calling you to a new obedience and trust in Him. And now a choice must be made: obedience or disobedience.

No team watches just one film and moves on. It is a continual process. Watch every game. Watch every play. Continue to grade your film with a trained eye and an accepting heart. Make it a regular part of your week. But don't fool yourself. Be honest and transparent with your evaluations and the standard God has called you to via His written word because partial obedience is not obedience.

The pages of this book are a call to obedience in many ways. But please know this as you prepare to close this book and move on. Heaven is not going to be a place where all the good people end up. Heaven is where all of the forgiven people end up. It's for those who have turned from their sin and trusted Jesus into their hearts.

No matter what your film reveals as of today, God loves you. His love is unconditional for you, and it's unconditional for me. As I have written this book, I have studied my own film closer than I ever have before. I see scars on my film that remind me of His healing power in my life. I notice I oftentimes walk with a limp due to the times I have fallen, but in the very next frame, I also see His hand is right there to pick me up. I see flaws, wounds, and hurts that have been covered up by God's grace and mercy to me. I am thankful for the scars, the limps, the flaws, and the hurts. For without them, I would not know who He truly is and how deeply he cares for me. My film doesn't lie. God loves you and He loves me more than any of us can possibly comprehend. It's an amazing love from a God who knows no limits in pursuing us, meeting us in our need, and leaving us forever changed. I pray every one of you will see something similar on your film: a God who never lets go of our hands, and may we never, ever let go of His.

ACKNOWLEDGMENTS

As many of you would expect, I am deeply grateful to my Lord and Savior Jesus Christ and for a Heavenly Father that has never let go of my hand. His love for me, His patience with me, His hand of provision, forgiveness, and protection over me has brought change to my heart, and I am forever grateful.

Thank you to Thomas J. Winters of Winters and King Inc. for believing in this book from Day One. Your efforts as my agent and the hours of work that Debby Boyd put into this project are greatly appreciated.

I am exceptionally grateful for the team members that God has placed in my life that challenge me every day. From co-workers at ESPN to college coaches across the country and my closest friends in Arkansas, you know who you are, and there are way too many to list. But I love you and I so much appreciate your encouragement, your consistency in who you are, and the example you are to me for what an authentic walk with God looks like.

To my mom and dad, thank you for taking me to church when I was a little boy. You grounded me in my faith. Well done to you both. I love you.

And to my wife, Tiffany, and our daughter, Kennedy. This book would not have been written without you in my life. You both inspire me. Tiffany, your love and kindness to others is an uncommon gift from God. Thank you for the hours and hours you sat in my office in our home, proofreading this book, and providing me honest feedback. Thank you for marrying me.

Kennedy, I hope someday you will read parts of this book to your own children, and they will have a heart for God just like you do. Your future husband will have a 100-question quiz over the content of this book. Just kidding...sort of.

And to our great dog Eli, who laid at my feet every single day as I labored to write a book. I hope to someday be half the man you think I am. You are my forever dog—faithful until the end.

Finally, to the team at Triumph Books. Thank you for partnering with me on this project. You guys are the best.